Independent Judgment

and

Introspection

ALSO BY JERRY KIRKPATRICK

In Defense of Advertising:
Arguments from Reason, Ethical Egoism,
and Laissez-Faire Capitalism

Montessori, Dewey, and Capitalism:
Educational Theory for a
Free Market in Education

INDEPENDENT JUDGMENT

AND

INTROSPECTION

FUNDAMENTAL REQUIREMENTS
OF THE
FREE SOCIETY

JERRY KIRKPATRICK

KIRKPATRICK BOOKS
UPLAND, CALIFORNIA

Publisher's Cataloging-in-Publication Data

Name: Kirkpatrick, Jerry, author.
Title: Independent judgment and introspection : fundamental
    requirements of the free society / Jerry Kirkpatrick.
Description: Upland, CA : Kirkpatrick Books, 2019. | Includes
    bibliographical references and index.
Identifiers: LCCN 2018913156 | ISBN 978-0-9787803-5-7
    (hardcover) | ISBN 978-0-9787803-6-4 (paperback) | ISBN
    978-0-9787803-7-1 (ebook)
Subjects: LCSH: Critical thinking. | Thought and
    thinking. | Autonomy (Psychology) | Introspection. |
    Human behavior. | Cognitive psychology. | BISAC:
    PSYCHOLOGY / Cognitive Psychology & Cognition. |
    PSYCHOLOGY / Developmental / General.
Classification: LCC BF316 .K57 2019 (print) | LCC BF316
    (ebook) | DDC 153/.4—dc23

Library of Congress Catalog Card Number: 2018913156

Kirkpatrick Books (formerly TLJ Books), Upland, CA 91784
http://www.jkirkpatrick.net, jkirkpa380@gmail.com

Printed in the United States of America

To Edith Packer (1924 – 2018)

Contents

Preface

The boy in the Hans Christian Andersen tale of "The Emperor's New Clothes" is often admired for his independent judgment, that is, for his courage to speak a truth that the adults feared to acknowledge openly. Two questions, however, can be asked about independent judgment as a character and personality trait. One, can everyone really practice it (besides naïve children) or is it the province of true creators and innovators, such as Socrates and Galileo? And, perhaps giving rise to doubts expressed in the first question, a second asks, how does one handle the hazards of independent judgment, such as the prospect of offending other people, sometimes resulting in death (Socrates) or house arrest (Galileo)?

Independent judgment is correct perception of the facts of reality and courage to acknowledge and assert those facts. The two questions above arise because of complicating factors; intelligence and interest can affect one's initial perception of facts and other people can affect both the initial perception and assertion of the judgment. Psychology plays a dominant role throughout.

Great innovators, especially those who challenge centuries of convention, are highly intelligent. They also are extremely interested and motivated in their areas of innovation. Those of us who do not possess the same intelligence or interest, whether college professor or blue-collar worker, can nevertheless use our intelligence in areas of interest to perceive and assert what we do see. Intelligence combined with interest determines who is likely to see ahead of others, and those of us who do not see initially can learn from those who do, but intelligence is not a prerogative of the highly educated. Independent judgment can be practiced equally by a garage door repairman as by a scientist.

So why don't more people practice independent judgment? Which is to ask, why don't they join the boy in the tale of "The Emperor's New Clothes"? The answer is fear, real or imagined, of what might happen to them. The real fear of death or incarceration that can result from speaking one's mind poses a needless moral quandary. We have no moral obligation to drink hemlock, as Socrates did, to preserve our independent judgment. Many in the Soviet Union managed to maintain theirs by expressing it to family and trusted friends, sometimes speaking in a foreign language to prevent nosy neighbors from overhearing their conversations and reporting them. They were conventional on the outside, in public, to preserve their lives, but independent on the inside, at home, to preserve their self-esteem.

Most of us do not face the real fears of a Socrates, Galileo, or citizen of the Soviet Union. Our fears of expressing independent judgment stem from what others might think of us. Disapproval, maybe rejection, is the worst that might happen, yet the anxiety caused by self-doubt can be so strong as to blur our perception of the facts, thus preventing any expression of an independent judgment. When choices based on self-doubt build up over time, habits of perceiving reality through clouded lenses become established patterns of behavior. Seeing the world through the eyes of others, whomever those significant others may be, becomes the norm. Conventionality is the result.

Can independent judgment be taught? Yes, but it must start at an early age. Children, of course, need to be given love and support, but they also need to be given freedom, within limits appropriate to their maturity, to choose their own values. And they need to be allowed to learn from their mistakes. Most parents are loving toward infants, but when the children move into their "terrible twos," parents begin controlling and in some cases hitting. Often, the controlling continues throughout childhood and becomes a constant in traditional schools.

Choice and self-assertion are seen as a disruption of authority and disobedience. In reality, they are signs of developing self-esteem and personal identity. When they are erased by the controlling, authoritarian behavior of adults, children quickly get the message that getting along means going along. It is a rare child who matures to adulthood with independent judgment intact. Perhaps this is why we tend to think that only certain people can fully achieve it.

Independent judgment is a fundamental requirement of the free society. Unless each adult citizen possesses a significant amount of self-esteem expressed as independent judgment, such a society cannot last.

The aim of this book is to explore the nature of independent judgment and its relationship to the free society. Throughout the journey, we will find that psychology, especially the skill of introspection, plays a significant role in developing and maintaining independence in the individual and in generating the desire to live in a free society.

The book begins by chronicling the historical war on independence, that is, how the character and personality trait has been ruthlessly destroyed in children from the earliest times of civilization and how it is routinely prevented from developing today. It next examines the nature of psychology as a science, psychology's epistemological foundations and its relation to political individualism and moral egoism. The book further analyzes how independent judgment develops in the individual, probing the depths of psychology to demonstrate how seemingly uncontrollable subconscious premises guide our lives and how we can identify and change those premises through introspection.

Several mistaken conceptions of independence are discussed, including the Socrates question, "do we have to die for our independence?" along with a clarification of the meanings of autonomy and responsibility, the relation of independence to intelligence and epistemological certainty, and a comment on three well-known deference to authority studies from the mid-twentieth century. Finally, the book elaborates the meaning of introspection and the defensive habits we must identify and correct through introspective skill, and it then recommends to parents and teachers methods of teaching that skill to their children and students. The overall aim of "educating for independence," as the last chapter is titled, is to correct, and preferably prevent, thinking errors that lead to psychological problems.

It is those psychological problems that prevent the development of independence and happiness and, in turn, the uncompromising desire to live in a totally free society. Independent judgment and introspection in each individual are the fundamental requirements of expanding personal and political freedom.

This work presupposes a context. On its most fundamental level, the context is the philosophy of Ayn Rand, especially her epistemology, though the rest of her philosophy also permeates the book's content. Deriving from Rand's philosophy, Nathaniel Branden provides the foundation of a psychology of self-esteem.

My most significant personal and professional influence over the forty-eight years that I knew her is psychologist Edith Packer, to whom this book has been dedicated. I knew Dr. Packer initially as my therapist, coach, and mentor, then as a personal friend. Her influence on this work is nearly total, the impetus being her lecture on "The Psychological Requirements of a Free Society." The two requirements, she states, are a strong sense of personal identity, which means self-esteem, and an equally strong willingness to take personal responsibility for one's life, that is, independence. It was her understanding of Ayn Rand's philosophy and application of the philosophy to her own approach to psychology—especially her concepts of core and mid-level evaluations and the art of introspection—that gave me the background and confidence to relate psychological independence to the free society and offer a defense of both as an integrated whole.

Without ignoring the role of volition in forming and correcting one's psychology, or the significance of reason and objectivity in maintaining mental health, Dr. Packer successfully removed the moralistic edge that, unfortunately, somewhat overshadows Ayn

Rand's writing (and Nathaniel Branden's early writings, including *The Psychology of Self-Esteem*, which Branden acknowledges in his preface to the book's 2001 edition).

As a psychotherapist, Dr. Packer described herself as "a friend for hire," which she indeed was. In her practice she treated people from all philosophies of life, but to students of Ayn Rand she always emphasized that it was not appropriate to live one's life imitating a character in a novel. We all must choose our own values, she said, and live our own lives—as independent, self-responsible individuals.

Psychology and psychotherapy belong to what are called the "helping professions." Dr. Packer was the master helper.

A major influence on Dr. Packer as a psychotherapist and on her decision to leave a law practice to become a psychotherapist was psychiatrist Allan Blumenthal. I would be remiss if I did not also acknowledge Dr. Blumenthal as a significant influence on my understanding of psychology. The free society depends on a sound theory of economics, so Ludwig von Mises and George Reisman, as in my previous two books, remain my primary influences.

My final two acknowledgments are to my wife, Linda Reardan, and our daughter, Thea. Linda has read, and contributed much to, the entire manuscript. Without her counsel, it could not have been written. Thea, throughout my work on this book, has rapidly grown into a self-responsible, psychologically independent and flourishing young adult. Both Linda and Thea have been exceedingly encouraging.

The usual disclaimers, of course, apply here that all responsibility for what I have written is mine.

Finally, a note on notes. This is a scholarly book, so the notes are meant to be read. In the hardcover and paperback editions, the notes are at the foot of the page where they belong. I include, insofar as possible, a "first published in" date (or "repr." after the original year of publication), something I would rather not have to look up when I read scholarly works. Apologies to those of you who have eyes like mine, which means I sometimes find it frustratingly difficult to find superscripted note numbers in the middle of a paragraph in the middle of a page. In the electronic versions the notes are readily clickable in both directions; finding a full citation should be scrollable or clickable, one can hope, without too much aggravation.

I have generally followed the "Notes and Bibliography" chapter of the *Chicago Manual of Style*, so shortened citations are used after the initial complete reference. A full bibliography repeats the essential data. I have also tried to follow Carol Fisher Saller's advice in *The Subversive Copy Editor*, namely, to park the schoolmarm's ruler and focus on clarity and consistency (without becoming slave to the latter).

Independent Judgment

and

Introspection

1

The War on Independence

The history of childhood has been a nightmare from which we have only recently begun to awaken. The further back in history one goes, the lower the level of child care, and the more likely children are to be killed, abandoned, beaten, terrorized and sexually abused.

—Lloyd deMause[1]

The most *selfish* of all things is the independent mind that recognizes no authority higher than its own and no value higher than its judgment of truth.

—John Galt[2]

MOST PARENTS AND TEACHERS TODAY in Western cultures want their charges to grow up to be independent, at least in a rudimentary sense. That has not always been the case.

The basic requirements of adulthood are the ability to support oneself after leaving home and school and a modicum of rationality or sensibility when making life's decisions, that is, not being impulsive or acting on whim. We would like to see our children and students make

---

[1] Lloyd deMause, "The Evolution of Childhood," in *The History of Childhood: The Untold Story of Child Abuse*," ed. Lloyd deMause (New York: Peter Bedrick Books, 1988), 1. First published in 1974.

[2] Ayn Rand, *Atlas Shrugged* (New York: Random House, 1957), 1030 (Rand's italics). Galt is the hero of Rand's novel.

sound judgments after weighing the evidence. We would like to see them pursue a career they enjoy, find a loving spouse, and, if they so choose, raise one or more children to a similar, responsible adulthood. We want sound, not necessarily independent, judgment.

As a character and personality trait, independence throughout history has been equated to disobedience, insubordination, self-absorption, condescension, and, of course, selfishness. Children who exhibit such traits are scorned, ridiculed, spanked, abused both physically and emotionally, and far worse. A parochial school teacher recently said to a parent, "We both know what these kids need." The parent responded, "Love?" The teacher without missing a beat said, "Authority."

In the not too distant past of the Christian Middle Ages, children were referred to as "filthy bundles of original sin" and "young vipers."[3] Abandonment of children and infanticide were common in the ancient world, continuing through the Middle Ages until about two hundred years ago. Corporal punishment, though declining, continues today, as do child enslavement and "honor" killings in some cultures.[4] In the latter cultures, respect for individuals and their independent judgments is nearly non-existent. Independence in the past was not, and today still is not, an admired virtue or personality trait.

THE ROOT OF DICTATORSHIP

The root of dictatorship is the parent-child relationship, stemming from the millenniums old theory of parenting and teaching based on authoritarianism. If it is okay to coerce children, why should it not also be okay to coerce adults?

---

[3] Colin Heywood, *A History of Childhood: Children and Childhood in the West from Medieval to Modern Times* (Cambridge, UK: Polity Press, 2001), 22. "We are born between feces and urine" is a statement that has been attributed to St. Augustine, but the quotation is disputed. "Augustine of Hippo," Wikiquote, last modified January 29, 2019, https://en.wikiquote.org/wiki/Augustine_of_Hippo.

[4] As of 2019, fifty-four countries have banned corporal punishment in all settings, including the home. The United States is not one of them. *Global Initiative to End All Corporal Punishment.* Accessed February 8, 2019. https://endcorporalpunishment.org/countdown/.

I drew this conclusion not just from the work of Maria Montessori,[5] but also from Haim Ginott,[6] Thomas Gordon,[7] Alfie Kohn,[8] and William Glasser.[9] All are advocates in varying degrees of intrinsic motivation. Some have even suggested a connection between external control psychology and dictatorship, as well as internal control and the free society, though none has linked the free society to laissez-faire capitalism. Psychiatrist Glasser goes furthest by commenting extensively on our "external control society" and the need for less of it. Glasser indeed provides a simple and fundamental foundation of my statement in his discussions of choice theory versus external control.

Choice theory, according to Glasser, means that we choose most of our behavior, including the mental illness of depression. Glasser prefers verbs to nouns, emphasizing what we choose to do rather than dwelling on what we think is done to us. So, he says that we do not suffer depression. Rather, we depress, or choose to depress, when we experience a disappointment. The way out of depressing, he says, is to take internal control of our lives by making value judgments to choose other, happier behaviors and then acting on those judgments.[10]

The broader implication, short of using physical force to exert power over others, is that we control only our own behaviors and not that of others. Even though we may try at length to change other people's behaviors, the result on our part is usually frustration, or worse, and on the part of the person we are trying to change resistance, rebellion, resignation, or withdrawal. The relationship—whether it is between parent and child, husband and wife, teacher and student, or manager

[5] Maria Montessori, *The Montessori Method*, trans. Anne E. George (1912; repr., New York: Schocken Books, 1964). First published in Italian in 1909.

[6] Haim G. Ginott, *Between Parent & Child: New Solutions to Old Problems* (New York, Macmillan, 1965).

[7] Thomas Gordon, *Parent Effectiveness Training: The Tested Way to Raise Responsible Children*, (1970; rev. ed., New York: Three Rivers Press, 2000).

[8] Alfie Kohn, *Punished by Rewards: The Trouble with Gold Stars, Incentive Plans, A's, Praise, and Other Bribes* (Boston: Houghton Mifflin, 1993).

[9] William Glasser, *Choice Theory: A New Psychology of Personal Freedom* (New York: HarperPerennial, 1999).

[10] Glasser, *Choice Theory*, chap. 1.

and employee—ultimately ends in unhappiness, and sometimes separation. The solution, says Glasser, is to stop trying to change other
people's behavior, acknowledging and acting on the fact that we can
only control or change our own.

This means avoiding Glasser's seven deadly habits that destroy
personal relationships: criticizing, blaming, complaining, nagging,
threatening, punishing, and bribing (rewarding to control).[11] These
are all tools of external control psychology and their aim is to coerce
behavioral change by bypassing the other person's consent or understanding. Criticizing and blaming, says Glasser, are the worst, though
all the habits erode closeness. When the aim of coercive behavioral
change is taken to the extreme, direct physical force may result, such
as spanking, beating, or the use of sticks, belts, and other weapons.
Caring, trusting, listening, supporting, negotiating, befriending, and
encouraging are the connecting habits that Glasser recommends as
replacements for the deadly ones.[12]

External control psychology is the belief that we know what is best
for others and that we have the right to impose our will on them. It
is the use of rewards and punishments as motivation. When elevated
to the relationship of politician and citizen—Glasser does not go this
far—external control psychology becomes the right to impose, by legislation or fiat, laws, regulations, and other edicts to force citizens
to do or not do what the politicians think is best. External control
psychology assumes, and attempts to invoke, dependence. It is the
real root of dictatorship.

Internal control psychology, on the other hand, is the foundation
of independent judgment. It assumes that each of us controls our own
destiny by choosing our values and behaviors. Interaction with others is conducted through reason and logic, that is, persuasion, rather

---

[11] William Glasser, *Unhappy Teenagers: A Way for Parents and Teachers to Reach
Them* (New York: HarperCollins, 2002), 13.

[12] Glasser, *Unhappy Teenagers*, 14. "When you stop controlling, you gain control"
is Glasser's advice to unhappy parents who keep trying to coerce and micromanage their rebellious teenagers. Glasser, 1–10.

than Glasser's manipulative deadly habits. Motivating others requires appealing to their self-interest, communicating in such a way that the others see benefit to themselves of the requested action. Internal control psychology treats others with dignity. It derives from a high level of self-esteem and respect for others and acknowledges that the others have or are capable of a similar disposition.

At the political level, internal control psychology means each individual has the right to choose and not be controlled or coerced by anyone else. To politicians and government in general, it means: leave us alone. Internal control psychology is the root of capitalism.

CHILD ABUSE

In *Montessori, Dewey, and Capitalism*[13] I first suggested that the root of dictatorship is the parent-child relationship.[14]

My comment, however, was probably too tame and needlessly cautious. Alice Miller, Lloyd deMause, and Bruce Perry, at least by implication, make the assertion clearer.

In the Name of Good Child Rearing

Miller, a Swiss psychologist (and former psychoanalyst), provides the strongest link in her book *For Your Own Good*,[15] in which she quotes the untranslated German text *Schwarze Pädagogik*,[16] a collection of extensive excerpts from child-rearing and educational guidebooks of eighteenth- and nineteenth-century Germany. The books and

---

[13] Jerry Kirkpatrick, *Montessori, Dewey, and Capitalism: Educational Theory for a Free Market in Education* (Claremont, CA: TLJ Books, 2008), 117.

[14] Restraining children who are about to harm themselves or others is not parental coercion. It is a defensive use of force, not its initiation, and it is protective of the well-being of the child and others.

[15] Alice Miller, *For Your Own Good: Hidden Cruelty in Child-Rearing and the Roots of Violence*, trans. Hildegard and Hunter Hannum (New York: Farrar Straus Giroux, 1983). First published in German in 1980.

[16] Katharina Rutschky, *Schwarze Pädagogik: Quellen zur Naturgeschichte der bürgerlichen Erziehung* (Berlin: Ullstein Buchverlage GmbH & Co. KG / Ullstein Tas, 1977). Literal translation of the title is "Black Pedagogy: Sources for the Natural History of Civic Education."

child-rearing ordeals are referred to in Miller's English translation as "poisonous pedagogy."[17]

The upshot of advice from this period is to break the child's will, to beat the wickedness—which usually means the budding assertiveness and independence—out of the child, and to command strict, unquestioned obedience to authority (of the parent, teacher, and other adults). Miller quotes J. G. Krüger from 1752:

> The only vice deserving of blows is obstinacy. . . . Your son is trying to usurp your authority, and you are justified in answering force with force in order to insure his respect, without which you will be unable to train him. The blows you administer should not be merely playful ones but should convince him that you are his master. . . . This will rob him of his courage to rebel.[18]

In the course of enduring this brutality, shame, and humiliation, children are expected to thank their persecutors for the "discipline" and in some cases to kiss the hand that has just viciously beaten them. It is, after all, for their own good.

Even without these demands, Miller points out, abused children defend and cling to their abusive caregivers, because the small amount of caregiving they have received is all they know.

Adolf Hitler and all the leaders of Third Reich, says Miller, suffered this "pedagogy" and proudly passed it on to their children and subjects. Hitler often bragged of not flinching when his father repeatedly beat him. In *For Your Own Good*, and elsewhere, Miller extensively cites D. G. M. Schreber, whose nineteenth-century books on child-rearing, at least one of which went through forty editions, preached self-renunciation and self-denial. When Schreber's nanny, for example, fed his child

---

[17] Alice Miller is well known for her first book *The Drama of the Gifted Child*, also published under the more correct title *Prisoners of Childhood*. Its thesis is that childhood experiences, some (or many) of which may be traumatic, influence our adult behavior, trapping us in the futile pursuit of infantile needs that were not satisfied by our parents. *The Drama of the Gifted Child: The Search for the True Self*, rev. ed., trans. Ruth Ward (New York: Basic Books, 1997). First published in German in 1979. Miller was an influence on the so-called repressed- or recovered-memory movement of the 1980s and '90s, so she must be read carefully.

[18] Miller, *For Your Own Good*, 14–15.

before herself, he fired the nanny on the spot, thus sending a message to all of Germany that the goal of child-rearing is to gird children for a life of self-denial, to rid them of their alleged weaknesses. They must learn to sacrifice from the first day of infancy on, said Schreber.[19] With this kind of upbringing, asks Miller, is it any wonder that the German people became attached to Hitler as a father-substitute and were only too glad to obey his commands?

Lloyd deMause, psychoanalyst and founder of the *Journal of Psychohistory*, traces the bleak history of childhood. While his psychoanalytical jargon can become excessive, and some historians have questioned his findings, deMause's shocking historical facts are abundantly documented. Brutalization, terrorization, and sexual abuse were common in ancient and medieval times, with child maltreatment gradually improving over the centuries such that the above descriptions of German child-rearing are actually an advance over the past. Infanticide, for example, usually of baby girls, and usually by exposure, was practiced widely in ancient Greece and Rome. Throughout history, and in some cultures still today, fathers have held the right to view and treat their wives and children as property. In Rome, the right was codified; Roman fathers *by law* had the right to kill their children.[20]

DeMause was not one to lie down in the face of his academic critics. He called for proof of his errors, but no one came forth with evidence. Indeed, he showed how selectively historians pick their facts so as not to paint a negative picture of early and primitive human life, especially as it pertains to children.[21] It is no secret that the premises, political or otherwise, of historians determines what they will emphasize.[22] Not many of today's historians are advocates of capitalism,

---

[19]The incident is described in Alice Miller, "The Political Consequences of Child Abuse," *Journal of Psychohistory* 26, no. 2 (Fall 1998). http://psychohistory.com /articles/the-political-consequences-of-child-abuse/.

[20]Carl A. Mounteer, "Roman Childhood, 200 B.C. to A.D. 600," *Journal of Psychohistory* 14, no. 3 (Winter 1987), 233–56.

[21]Lloyd deMause, "On Writing Childhood History," *Journal of Psychohistory* 16, no. 2 (Fall 1988), 135–70.

[22]Roy A. Childs, Jr., "Big Business and the Rise of American Statism," in *Liberty*

which means not many are likely to present current civilization in a rosier light than that of the "good old days" of pre-capitalistic eras. Just look at the historians' romanticization of women and children before the industrial revolution and their alleged victimization during it, and then look at T. S. Ashton's factual retort.[23]

Even historian Heywood acknowledges that "we are bound to agree with Lloyd deMause that by the early twentieth century children in the West were less likely to be killed, abandoned or beaten than in the past."[24]

Although traumatic childhoods per se do not trump free will and deterministically turn children into dictators or sacrificial lambs, those experiences certainly make recovery difficult, and it would require an unusual child to break free of the circumstances. Bruce Perry, neurobiologist and psychiatrist, specializes in childhood trauma and neglect. He acknowledges (without endorsing free will or volition outright) that children do make thousands of decisions while growing up. It is those decisions, not genes or environment, that ultimately determine whether one neglected child (such as an infant left home alone every day for eight or more hours in a dark room) becomes a psychopathic killer and another an emotionless, socially awkward adolescent.[25]

Against Power: Essays by Roy A. Childs., Jr., ed. Joan Kennedy Taylor (San Francisco: Fox & Wilkes, 1994), 15–47. An earlier version of the essay was published in 1971 in *Reason* magazine. Childs uses familiar words from Ayn Rand's definition of art to define history as a "selective recreation of the events of the past, according to a historian's premises regarding what is important and his judgment concerning the nature of causality in human action." Childs, "Big Business," 18.

[23] T. S. Ashton, *The Industrial Revolution: 1760–1830* (1948; rev. ed., London: Oxford University Press, 1969). See also F. A. Hayek, ed., *Capitalism and the Historians* (Chicago: University of Chicago Press, 1954).

[24] Heywood, *A History of Childhood*, 116–17.

[25] Bruce D. Perry and Maia Szalavitz, *The Boy Who Was Raised as a Dog, and Other Stories from a Child Psychiatrist's Notebooks* (New York: Basic Books, 2006), 119–20. It should be emphasized at this point that trauma of any kind, whether sex abuse or the stress of wartime combat, is not forgotten or repressed. Therapists have their hands full helping patients cope with their omnipresent traumatic memories. Paul R. McHugh, *The Mind Has Mountains: Reflections on Society and Psychiatry* (Baltimore: Johns Hopkins University Press, 2006), 10–17. McHugh, *Try to Remember: Psychiatry's Clash Over Meaning, Memory, and Mind* (New York: Dana Press, 2008), 46. The "repressed" or "recovered" memory movement of the

To be sure, Perry insists, early discovery and non-drug, empathic psychotherapy are the remedies to such disturbances.[26] Trauma of any kind—and this includes spanking by hand—overloads the brain's stress response systems, causing a loss of felt control and competence by the victim. That is, the trauma prevents or erodes the development of self-esteem and independence. It does not have to be physical force. Trauma can be emotional abuse brought about by raging insults, name-calling, and belittling, or the lack of nurturing warmth, hugs, and understanding. Neglect, Perry points out, is not the prerogative of the poor and uneducated. There are also many uncared-for infants, children, and adolescents among the educated well-off.

For as far back as we can go in history, children—at least those who have been allowed to live—have been beaten by their caregivers, abused, manipulated, and commanded to obey authority. Obedience and independence are opposites. A parent-child relationship that commands blind obedience from the child is one that prepares the way for dictatorship. A free society thrives on independence; it requires a healthy disrespect of authority, which is acquired through nurturing, warm, and affectionate caregiving. Coercion of any kind, physical or emotional, in the parent-child relationship must be eliminated.

1980s and '90s, that is, the alleged, but false, memories of sex abuse sometimes alleged to manifest themselves in later life as "multiple personality disorders" or "dissociation," was brought about by "Manneristic Freudians," to use McHugh's words, who almost from the beginning of therapy would suggest to suggestible people in need of help that they were victims of unremembered sex abuse. The "recovered memories," McHugh argues, were in fact products of pathological hysteria, the same syndrome that Freud treated in his day and the same syndrome that gave us the Salem witch trials. McHugh, *Try to Remember*, 33–35 and chap. 10. Unfortunately, the repressed-memory movement is still alive today. See Mark Pendergrast, *Memory Warp: How the Myth of Repressed Memory Arose and Refuses to Die* (Hinesburg, VT: Upper Access Books, 2017).

[26] Perry and Szalavitz, *Boy Raised as a Dog*, 125–34. The title story in Perry's book is about a boy named Justin who lived in a kennel, in a dog cage, for five years. When taken to the hospital, he threw feces and food at the staff. Perry's empathic approach to therapy, however, reached him so that by age eight, Justin was able to enter kindergarten.

In the Name of Good Child Healthcare

"Children Don't Have Disorders; They Live in a Disordered World," say attention deficit hyperactivity disorder (ADHD) critics psychiatrist Peter Breggin and Ginger Ross Breggin.[27] Their comment is a variation of Maria Montessori's advice to "control the environment, not the child." For Montessori, children develop healthy psychologies, that is, become "normalized," to use her term, by being left free to pursue their own interests and choose their own educational work, provided the surroundings of the classroom are made safe and stimulating. Normalization leads to independence.[28]

Drugs, however, are a cruel and totally unwarranted control of the child.

Most children who exhibit the widely flaunted ADHD symptoms—inattention, hyperactivity, impulsiveness—are simply failing to handle the boredom, confusion, or authoritarianism, or all three, of school, home, and other environments in which they live and play.[29] They are not diseased kids, possessing neurological or biochemical imbalances, who require addicting, cocaine-like stimulants to cow them into submission. They are youngsters trying to learn and have fun in the process, but their world is complex and often the opposite of fun, especially school. What they desperately need is to be left free as much as possible to pursue their own interests and, when they request it, one or several adults to be their friends, to pay attention to them, to listen to their pleasures and worries, and to be their coach and confidant. What they decidedly do not need are Glasser's deadly habits. These habits, of

---

[27] Peter R. Breggin and Ginger Ross Breggin, "The Hazards of Treating 'Attention-Deficit/Hyperactivity Disorder' with Methylphenidate (Ritalin)," *Journal of College Student Psychotherapy* 10, no. 2 (1995), 69.

[28] Maria Montessori, *Spontaneous Activity in Education*, trans. Florence Simmonds (1917; repr., Cambridge, MA: Robert Bentley, 1971), 71. First published in Italian in 1916. Montessori, *The Absorbent Mind*, trans. Claude A. Claremont (1949; repr., New York: Henry Holt & Company, 1995), 201–07, 223. First published in Italian in 1949.

[29] I say "confusion" because some parents today who have rejected the authoritarianism of their parents and grandparents have nevertheless failed to provide structure and consistency for their children. Similar behavior can result. Some schools can also provide this confusion.

course, are staples of their world, and ours, but many children do not know how to cope with them. What they do not need is to be made to feel stoned or spaced out.

Labeling children with ADHD stigmatizes them as inadequate and, as a result, induces unearned guilt, because the adults who recommend the drugs are blaming them for their behavior even though the theory behind the whole psychotropic drug mantra is materialism and determinism. A child who acts up in class, or who does not pay attention, according to the adults, must be controlled. Something, so the adults say, is wrong with the child, not with the adults' methods of relating to the child. The message is clear.

Montessori entrepreneur and master teacher Donna Bryant Goertz says that medication today is the new spanking. The purpose of the drugs is submission and control.[30]

The evidence for a physiological basis of ADHD behavior does not exist. The experimental studies do not uphold the belief. This is especially confirmed when the ADHD researchers themselves admit that the children improve during summer vacation and when taught in smaller, more attention-focused classes.[31]

The criteria for parents to look at concerning ADHD are Glasser's. If your child, says Glasser, can watch and understand television, play video games, and use a computer, do better for some teachers than for others, do better in one subject than another that requires the same level of reading and understanding, and has good friends he or she enjoys being with, then it is highly unlikely that there is anything wrong with your child.[32] Glasser piercingly and humorously puts the issue in perspective when he says that the worst attention deficit disorders in the world are husbands and wives, because many of them so often do not listen to each other! Glasser also calls psychotropic medicines "brain drugs," refusing to grant them the honorific "medicine," and refers to

---

[30] Donna Bryant Goertz, *Children Who Are Not Yet Peaceful: Preventing Exclusion in the Early Elementary Classroom* (Berkeley, CA: Frog Books, 2001), 16.

[31] Breggin and Breggin, "The Hazards of Treating," 58–61.

[32] Glasser, *Choice Theory*, 255–59.

their side effects as *effects*. There's nothing secondary or "side," he says, about the effects of brain drugs.

Many so-called problem children are just bored of sitting at a desk in a classroom and sick of having adults lord their size and power over them. What they need is an empathic friend or sometimes to be left alone, perhaps to go fish. The alternative, Summerhill-like Sudbury Valley School in Framingham, Massachusetts, does not schedule or require regular classes, but it does have a pond on its property and students are allowed to go fishing all day if they so desire. "Going fishing" is not possible at most schools in the world today, but it does make a good metaphor for getting adults off the backs of children and, more generally, for removing confusion and authoritarianism from their lives.

Sudbury Valley does not have an ADHD problem among its students. Its goal is to teach independence.[33]

ADULT ABUSE

It is no accident that Thomas Hobbes—he's the one who said life in a state of nature is "solitary, poor, nasty, brutish, and short"—advocated dictatorship. He was a materialist and therefore a determinist. Materialism is the philosophical notion that consciousness is an illusion, at best an effect or by-product of the brain that causes nothing. Materialism denies free will and therefore assumes that all our behavior is determined either by internal bodily functions or by external environmental events, or some combination. The mind plays no role in influencing behavior. To avoid living in a nasty, brutish, anarchical society, says Hobbes, we need a strong, controlling central authority—the sovereign power of the "public sword"—to tell us what to do. Independence is not welcomed in a controlled society.[34]

---

[33]Daniel Greenberg, *The Crisis in American Education* (Framingham, MA: Sudbury Valley School Press, 1970), 53–55. Greenberg, *Free at Last: The Sudbury Valley School* (Framingham, MA: Sudbury Valley School Press, 1987), 37–39, 109–13. Mimsy Sadofsky and Daniel Greenberg, eds., *Reflections on the Sudbury School Concept* (Framingham, MA: The Sudbury Valley School Press, 1999), 268–75.

[34]Thomas Hobbes, *Leviathan or the Matter, Forme, & Power of a Common-wealth Ecclesiasticall and Civill* (London: Andrew Crooke, 1651), 28, 78, 106–108.

Today, many scientists are materialists and determinists.

And today, the field of psychiatry exemplifies all too well the theoretical dominance of materialism and determinism. Many of its practitioners have no qualms about imprisoning people against their will, then forcibly giving them electro-convulsive shock treatments or psychotropic drugs, or performing surgery on them. The coercion is considered good medical practice, made possible by government-sanctioned licensing and patent monopolies, the government socialized and cartelized medical-insurance system, and laws regulating both state-run and private mental hospitals and wards. The effects of the treatments are not cures for "biochemical imbalances," as the physiological psychiatrists describe mental illness. They amount to total control over unwanted behaviors and the ultimate consequences of the treatments often are irreversible brain and body damage.

In the Name of Good Science

One of the many tragic ironies in the history of science is the story of Ignác Semmelweis, an independent personality who discovered the significance of and recommended—futilely in his lifetime—the use of antiseptic procedures in childbirth.

Semmelweis died a brutal death in an insane asylum.

Suffering in 1865, probably from Alzheimer's disease, though some historians suspect syphilis, he was deceptively lured to a mental hospital. When he tried to leave, he was severely beaten, dying two weeks later of septicemia, or blood poisoning, which he had argued was the cause of childbed fever. Such poisoning, he said, can be prevented by having all doctors and assistants wash their hands in chlorinated water.[35]

The "Men of Hard Science." Beatings, straitjackets, dark cells, cold water, castor oil. These were common "treatments" of the insane in the nineteenth century. The twentieth and twenty-first centuries have not been much better.

---

[35] Sherwin B. Nuland, *The Doctors' Plague: Germs, Childbed Fever, and the Strange Story of Ignác Semmelweis* (New York: W. W. Norton, 2003).

Prior to the advent of the insane asylum, the mad were looked after in the homes of relatives or sent to a monastery, or locked in a tower or dungeon. The "great confinement," as Michel Foucault calls it, occurred in France in the seventeenth century, when leper colonies were emptied and replaced with the mad. Other historians note that this "confinement" varied by country and extended to as late as the mid-nineteenth century, but the pattern was the same: to remove the insane—and it did not always include only the insane—from society. Sometimes, unwanted wives or other supposedly embarrassing family members were confined to asylums. Therapeutic treatment was not the reason for separation.[36]

How were the insane handled? The fundamental premise at the time was that the insane were wild beasts that had to be put in cages and tamed; they were not considered human. Hence the prison-like atmosphere, restraints and beatings, blood-letting, spinning chairs, dunking in cold water to the point of nearly drowning, and administration of powerful emetics. These techniques were used repeatedly, day after day, sometimes for months. The aim of the mad-doctors, as psychiatrists were called prior to the late nineteenth century, was to terrorize patients, to break their will and supposedly knock the insanity out of them.

In the nineteenth century, however, there was a brief exception to the brutal "therapies." To be sure, many of the same cruel and inhumane techniques continued, but the Quakers, beginning in late eighteenth-century England and continuing in the United States during the nineteenth, created the "moral treatment" movement in mental health. Recognizing that mental illness was not physiological, that it resulted from being overwhelmed by certain life events, the Quakers insisted on kindness, attention, listening, and talking as keys to helping the mentally ill. A retreat or farm was often the place of aid.[37]

---

[36] Michel Foucault, *Madness & Civilization: A History of Insanity in the Age of Reason*, trans. Richard Howard (New York: Random House, 1965; repr. Vintage Books, 1973), 3–64. First published in French in 1964. Roy Porter, *Madness: A Brief History* (Oxford: Oxford University Press, 2001), 92–100.

[37] Porter, *Madness*, 104–108. Robert Whitaker, *Mad in America: Bad Science, Bad Medicine, and the Enduring Mistreatment of the Mentally Ill* (New York: Basic Books, 2002), 30–38.

One example is the Pennsylvania Hospital that opened outside of Philadelphia in 1841. Fed well and allowed to sew, garden, read, write, and play games, the patients enjoyed a "pastoral comfort." The hospital included a dining room, a greenhouse, a library, and a museum. The patients were encouraged to develop friendships, dress well, and rethink their behavior. They were urged to exercise free will and, not unlike Glasser's approach to counseling, *choose* to be sane, to recover their lost independence. They were neither chained nor beaten.

By 1890 all trace of moral treatment of the mentally ill was gone. The explosive growth of state-run, bureaucratized hospitals are said to have made it impossible to train attendants in the spirit of kindness and empathy. What really killed moral treatment, however, was the ridicule and condescension put forth by medical doctors, especially the neurologists. They all considered themselves to be "men of hard science," to use Robert Whitaker's phrase, and the moral treatment advocates were just old-fashioned, religious "gardeners and farmers." In the name of science straitjackets and cruelty were brought back; kindness and empathy were out.[38]

The Medical Model. The "men of hard science"—and today, of course, there are many "women of hard science"—gave us the medical model of psychiatry.

The story is documented in Peter Breggin's 1991 book *Toxic Psychiatry* and Robert Whitaker's 2010 text *Anatomy of an Epidemic.*[39] The medical model says psychological problems such as anxiety, depression, schizophrenia, and whatever else shuts down our quest for independence and happiness are physiologically based and must be treated medically, that is, with electroshock, drugs, or surgery. (And psychosurgery, though not usually called lobotomy today, is still practiced in

---

[38] Whitaker, *Mad in America*, 37.

[39] Peter R. Breggin, *Toxic Psychiatry: Why Therapy, Empathy, and Love Must Replace the Drugs, Electroshock, and Biochemical Theories of the "New Psychiatry"* (New York: St. Martin's Press, 1991). Robert Whitaker, *Anatomy of an Epidemic: Magic Bullets, Psychiatric Drugs, and the Astonishing Rise of Mental illness in America* (New York: Broadway Paperbacks, 2010).

the twenty-first century.[40]) Courses on psychotherapy, Breggin points out, are no longer taught in many medical schools to train psychiatrists in an empathic approach to counseling. To materialists and determinists this makes sense; when a pill or other physiological treatment can be given to cure sickness, talk therapy is useless.

Yet there is no scientifically valid evidence for the physiological cause of most mental problems. There is a great deal of evidence that the medical model causes physiological and psychological harm.

In page after page, chapter after chapter, Breggin cites researchers, many of them psychiatrists, who acknowledge that no causal connection has been demonstrated between brain physiology and psychological problems. Quite the contrary, evidence of brain damage due to electroshock, drugs, and surgery is abundant. For example, tardive dyskinesia and brain shrinkage are two common effects of the typical "treatments." The terms "chemical straitjacket" and "chemical lobotomy" are used by psychiatrists to describe the results of drug use and the immediate, short-term effect of drugs (and shock and surgery) is described as "blunting the personality," "flattened affect," and "subdued behavior." The patients, in other words, look and act drugged.

The "treatments" are instruments of restraint, especially of the more hyperactive personalities; they are used not just in mental wards, but also in prisons and, as noted above, in schools. Breggin calls psychotropic drugs "neurotoxins," because they poison the brain.[41]

Whitaker provides updates to Breggin with, at times, focused technical discussions made readily understandable to the layperson. For example, the chemical imbalance theory of psychological disorders claims that the depressive's brain has too little serotonin and the schizophrenic's too much dopamine. Thus, the medical "solution" should be

---

[40] Adriana Barton, "Study Renews Debate about Surgical Treatment for Psychiatric Disorders," *The Globe and Mail*, June 6, 2013, https://www.theglobeandmail.com/.

[41] Throughout his career, Breggin has exhibited exceptional courage and independence—in 1973 by unflinchingly denouncing in the face of threats the psychosurgery profession and in 1987 by defeating an attempt to revoke his license. Peter Breggin, "Alert 22: Threatening to 'Get Breggin!'" *Psychiatric Drug Facts*. Accessed February 8, 2019, https://breggin.com/alert-22-threatening-to-get-breggin/.

to increase the serotonin in the depressive and decrease dopamine in the schizophrenic. But the drugs don't work and usually cause additional harm to the patients' brains.

Whitaker cites numerous researchers. One anti-drug psychiatrist says, "The serotonin theory of depression is comparable to the [older, now discredited] masturbatory theory of insanity."[42] And a neuroscientist concludes, "The evidence does not support any of the biochemical theories of mental illness."[43] In contrast, confirming Breggin's earlier statements, long-term drug use has led to tardive dyskinesia, frontal lobe shrinkage, and permanent psychosis. Withdrawal from long-term use has led to tics and agitation, including thoughts of violence and suicide, some of which are occasionally implemented.

The solution to mental difficulties is mental, that is, the correction of mistakes that have been made in one's thinking; it begins with Carl Rogers' fundamental premise of an "unconditional positive regard" toward anyone in need of help and a nurturing, empathic conversation.[44] Indeed, safe houses have been run successfully by amateurs—psychiatric survivors in some cases—and have produced better results for schizophrenics than any of the shocks, drugs, or surgeries of psychiatrists. As William Glasser puts it, schizophrenics are "just lonely people" who need a friend.[45] Breggin concurs that the root of serious psychological problems most often is to be found in dysfunctional family and personal relationships.[46]

---

[42]Quoted in Whitaker, *Anatomy of an Epidemic*, 75.

[43]Quoted in Whitaker, *Anatomy of an Epidemic*, 78. See https://www.madinamerica.com/science-of-psychiatric-drugs/ for detailed listings of scholarly literature on the shortcomings of psychotropic drug use.

[44]Carl Rogers, *On Becoming a Person: A Therapist's View of Psychotherapy* (New York: Houghton Mifflin, 1961), 61–62. Freud seems to have been empathic, though some of his followers may not have been.

[45]I was in Glasser's presence when he made this statement. Glasser, though, does not mean that some schizophrenics and psychotics will not need short-term doses of sedative drugs to calm them before talk therapy can occur. See Glasser, *Choice Theory*, 136, 147–49.

[46]World Health Organization cross-cultural studies in 1969, 1978, 1997 have shown that medicated schizophrenic patients in the United States and five other developed countries fared worse—short term and long term—than the mostly

Why do establishment psychiatrists persist in using the medical model when the evidence against it continues to pile up? Materialism, of course, is no lightweight theory, and it blinds psychiatrists to the contents of consciousness and possible psychological causes of mental distress. As academic researchers, some psychiatrists do what other academics have been known to do when discovering embarrassing facts: they bury them in footnotes (found by Breggin) or relegate their confessions and cautions to post-research interviews (all, again, found by Breggin) long after the headlines of supposed drug success have played out in the press. And then there's the blatant conflict of interest, acknowledged by too few psychiatrists, of the millions of pharmaceutical company dollars that are fed to the profession.

"Modern psychiatry," as Breggin puts it, "is not about counseling and empowering people. It's about controlling and suppressing them."[47] Psychiatry's history, says John Read, dates to the seventeenth century but its tactics too often over the years have been those of the Inquisition: subjugating "behaviours unacceptable or inconvenient to those in power."[48] Mental hospitals of the nineteenth century, and even of the twentieth, have been called "snake pits"; inmates then, and still today, were and are treated as objects, not people with problems to be resolved.

---

un-medicated patients in India, Nigeria, and Columbia. Whitaker, *Anatomy of an Epidemic*, 110–11. In Tornio, Finland, "open-dialogue" family-centered therapy has reduced first-episode schizophrenia by 90% since the 1980s. Psychotic symptoms often retreat within a month and drugs are seldom used. If necessary, drugs are used in modest dosages and for a short term. One ward of the hospital is empty because schizophrenia is disappearing from the region. Whittaker, *Anatomy of an Epidemic*, 336–44. For a detailed analysis and review of research supporting the thesis that mental illness is cognitive, not physiological, see Richard P. Bentall, *Madness Explained: Psychosis and Human Nature* (London: Penguin Books, 2003).

[47] Peter R. Breggin, "The Fort Hood Shooter: A Different Psychiatric Perspective," *Huffpost Politics*, May 25, 2011, https://www.huffingtonpost.com/dr-peter-breggin/the-fort-hood-shooter-a-d_b_349651.html.

[48] John Read, "A History of Madness," in John Read and Jacqui Dillon, eds., *Models of Madness: Psychological, Social and Biological Approaches to Psychosis*, 2nd ed. (New York: Routledge, 2013), 14. The 2004 edition of *Models of Madness* sold over 11,000 copies, an impressive number for a scholarly collection that challenges the premises of the medical model.

Thomas Szasz, early and vocal critic of the medical model, likened the questionable science of modern psychiatry to alchemy and astrology.[49] Perhaps it should be called totalitarian science. Szasz argued that involuntary treatment, such as electroshock and psychosurgery, meets the definition of torture. Independence is not the medical model's goal.

The Progressives' Eugenics Episode. Another "science" that should be called totalitarian, or at least led in a straight line to totalitarianism, was eugenics, bipartisan guiding light of early twentieth-century American and English politics. The US episode is chronicled in detail by Whitaker and Thomas C. Leonard.[50]

The word "eugenics" was coined by Francis Galton and the field was considered state-of-the-art science from about 1890 to 1930. "Well-born" is its meaning and it assumes that the superior race must use hereditary controls—compulsory sterilization in the United States and United Kingdom and compulsory euthanasia in Nazi Germany— to protect the better race from dilution or contamination.[51] Inferiors

---

[49] Thomas Szasz, *The Myth of Mental Illness: Foundations of a Theory of Personal Conduct*, 2nd ed. (New York: Harper Perennial, 1974), 1. First edition published in 1961 with the subtitle: *A Critical Assessment of the Freudian Approach*. First statement of the myth was expressed in Thomas Szasz, "The Myth of Mental Illness," *American Psychologist* 15 (1960), 113–18, https://dx.doi.org/10.1037/h0046535. By "mental illness," Szasz means disease of the brain, or physiological disorder, such as syphilis or epilepsy, and such sufferers should be referred to a physician, especially a neurologist, not a psychiatrist or psychologist. Mental distress, or "problems in living," to use Szasz's words, is the affliction the psychotherapist seeks to allay.

[50] Whitaker, *Mad in America*, 42–45, 52–56. Thomas C. Leonard, *Illiberal Reformers: Race, Eugenics and American Economics in the Progressive Era* (Princeton, NJ: Princeton University Press, 2016).

[51] For the Nazi connection, see Peter R. Breggin, "Psychiatry's Role in the Holocaust," *International Journal of Risk & Safety in Medicine* 4 (1993), 133–48. The eugenics episode is seldom talked about today or taught in schools, for the obvious reason of its link to current Progressive politics. Even less talked about is the role of American psychiatrists in promoting and supporting the Nazi sterilization program (1934–39). German psychiatrists advocated euthanasia of the developmentally retarded and mentally defective, and in 1938 began ordering "mercy killings" in gas chambers disguised as showers. By 1941, the death chambers were used for the Holocaust. See also John Read and Jeffrey Masson, "Genetics, Eugenics and Mass Murder," in *Models of Madness*, 34–46. Euthanasia continued to be advocated by American psychiatrists in 1942. Jay Joseph, "The 1942 'Euthanasia' Debate in the *American Journal of Psychiatry*," *History of Psychiatry*, 16, no. 2 (2005), 171–79, https://dx.doi.org/10.1177/0957154X05047004.

included the disabled, the feeble minded, the insane, immigrants from Asia and southern and eastern Europe, African Americans, Jews, and women. The "superiors" in the United States at the time were mostly evangelical white Anglo-Saxon Protestant males; they were trained in German universities in democratic socialism. Their goal was to establish an administrative state of scientific experts, "more Bismarckian than Marxian," as Leonard puts it, to dictate over and micromanage modern society.[52]

Eugenics elitism and racism died with the Nazis, which means it was not an essential characteristic of early Progressivism, but it did fit the Progressives' program. And that program was to use a form of Darwinian science, supported by materialism and determinism, to defeat the individualism of laissez-faire capitalism and its proponents, who at the time were the classical liberals Herbert Spencer and William Graham Sumner. On moral grounds, because laissez-faire was considered un-Christian, which meant selfish, the Progressives' goal was to make society more efficient, guided by the "natural aristocrats" working in government bureaus. Hence, the birth, during that period, and explosive growth of regulatory agencies, along with think tanks to advise the "experts" running the agencies. The public good, as "discovered" and defined by the experts, supplanted individual rights.[53]

Thus, the ancient metaphor of the organic theory of society ruled supreme as a significant component of the Progressive program. It is still with us today. According to the metaphor, if certain cells of the body (politic) are deemed by experts to be inferior or even defective, they must be controlled and treated, or removed from society (to a

---

[52] Thomas C. Leonard, "American Reform in the Progressive Era: Its Foundational Beliefs and Their Relation to Eugenics," *History of Political Economy* 41, no. 1 (2009), 116, https://dx.doi.org/10.1215/00182702-2008-040.

[53] "Social Darwinism" is a pejorative used by modern historians to denigrate the ideas of Spencer and Sumner, giving the impression that "social Darwinism" is what motivated the Progressives' opponents. The term, however, according to Leonard, is an invention of Richard Hofstadter in 1944. Leonard, "Origins of the Myth of Social Darwinism: The Ambiguous Legacy of Richard Hofstadter's *Social Darwinism in American Thought*," *Journal of Economic Behavior & Organization* 71 (2009), 37–51. https://doi.org/10.1016/j.jebo.2007.11.004.

home or asylum in the country), or sterilized or killed. More than 60,000 compulsory sterilizations were performed in the United States, as late as 1972. Minimum wage legislation was passed to exclude the least skilled from the work force, which included women and African Americans and the rest of the "inferiors" who were believed to be a threat to the jobs of superior Anglo-Saxon males. Immigration barriers, beginning with the Chinese Exclusion Act of 1882 and concluding with the Immigration Acts of 1917 and 1924, were imposed for the same reason: to freeze out the competition.[54]

Such heavy-handed control over society does not allow much chance of independence, unless one happens to be a white Anglo-Saxon Protestant male. The Progressives' administrative state is alive and well today, more Marxian and egalitarian, at least for certain "oppressed" groups, than Bismarckian. But the coercive hand of socialistic control and legal plunder has grown exponentially, making the achievement of independence more and more difficult. For the many who are offered a variety of free goods and services, better known as entitlements or welfare, socialistic control has made independence a dirty word. Why work or strive to improve oneself when the "experts" in government will give us everything we need?

But again, this is what materialism and determinism lead to: total, political domination. Consciousness is irrelevant, free will does not exist. Psychological causes of behavior are an illusion.

Hobbes was right. Dictatorship must follow from materialism and determinism. Independence is out.

In the Name of the Good

To obey an authority can mean to follow the instructions or direction of an accepted leader, such as a teacher, business manager, or orchestra conductor, but it usually means more.

---

[54]Leonard, *Illiberal Reformers*, 45, 142. Early feminists opposed minimum wage laws and the 8-hour day, because they were willing to work for less than the minimum and longer than 8-hours. The men did not approve. Leonard, *Illiberal Reformers*, 179–85.

In the past, to obey authority has meant, and today still means: without question or independent judgment, accept and perform commands issued by those in superior rank and power.[55] The highest rank and power over humans has been held by the concept of a supernatural being. The commandments in the Judeo-Christian Bibles, for example, are not items submitted by God for discussion or debate. They are deontological rules to be followed without regard for personal consequence. They are akin to the civil laws of the land; if not followed, violators are punished.

The flip side of materialism and determinism is a form of idealism. As the *Oxford English Dictionary* (OED) puts it, philosophical idealism means: "Reality is ultimately in some sense mental or mind-dependent; [idealism is] any of various views according to which the objects of knowledge or perception are ideas."[56] The religious form of the theory usually allows discussion of consciousness and free will, but at the expense of reason, science, and the natural world in which we live. The natural world, according to Plato, an idealist, and many religions, is said to be illusory and temporary. Our goal is to obey the rules of the religion so that when we die we will go to heaven and enjoy eternal bliss.

God. Throughout history the greatest enemy of independent judgment, and therefore the free society, has been and continues to be the belief in a supernatural being. Whatever is above or beyond nature means it is above and beyond humans, which means it is above reason, science, and logic. It means humans are inferior to the all-powerful and all-knowing god. The concept of a supreme being presupposes that humans are dependent on the god that is the creator and controller of the universe. There is no place for independence.

---

[55] The definition of "obey" in Webster's unabridged dictionary says: "to perform or behave as directed often without question or attempt at independent decision." And in its synonym discussion: "it may suggest lack of questioning and attempting independent judgment." *Webster's Third New International Dictionary, Unabridged,* s.v. "obey," accessed February 8, 2019, http://unabridged.merriam-webster.com.

[56] *Oxford English Dictionary Online,* s.v. "idealism," accessed February 8, 2019, http://www.oed.com.

What is the concept of god? Essentially, it is a consciousness projected by humans beyond and outside of themselves to provide causal explanations of natural phenomena and to grant wishes that may or may not be naturally feasible.

Evolving from the animism of earlier ages in which spirits were believed to exist in plants, animals, and inanimate matter, the notion of many gods, or polytheism, arose to indicate which ones could help or hurt one's life on earth. Many gods eventually led to competition for god in chief, so to speak, such as Zeus in Greek mythology. At some point, in various parts of the world, the concept of a single, all-powerful and all-knowing consciousness integrated all previous animistic and polytheistic conceptions into one. In this sense, monotheism was an advance for civilization, as it was a higher level of conceptualization than either animism or polytheism. It generally reduced magical thinking and control to the one giant consciousness in the sky, or rather, as philosophers and theologians put it, when they have chosen to state a location of the god, in some other dimension of reality.

This gives us philosophical and religious idealism, the doctrine that reality essentially is mental or mind-dependent, as the OED puts it, a reflection of the god's consciousness. What we perceive are ideas in the god's mind. Material, naturalistic reality is illusory. The giant consciousness in the sky does not allow humans to be independent, because we would not be here were it not for the god.

This can, but usually does not, mean that god is immanent in nature, which gives us pantheism. As George H. Smith says, "If god is taken to be synonymous with nature or some aspect of the natural universe, we may then ask why the term 'god' is used at all. It is superfluous and highly misleading. The label of 'god' serves no function."[57] The same can be said of the god of deism, the "scientist in chief," as it were, who created the universe, but does not interfere with its natural laws. The notion of such gods deflects attention from the tasks of living on earth. So do the notions of a supernatural and transcendent god.

---

[57] George H. Smith, *Atheism: The Case Against God* (1979; repr., Buffalo, NY: Prometheus Books, 1989), 32.

"Supernatural," as Smith continues in his analysis, means that the god is exempt from causal laws and can therefore interfere to do whatever it wants. Humans, in effect, must constantly look over their shoulders, lest something dire from on high happens to them, and they must constantly be aware that whatever they perceive may not really be so. "Transcendence" means the god is beyond human comprehension and therefore not capable of being known. Aside from raising the questions of "why bother?" and "how do you know?" to those who claim that god is transcendent, the concept of transcendence demotes the power and capability of human minds by implanting the premise of the unknowable. In both of these cases—of the supernatural and the transcendent—human cognition is devalued, which means self-esteem is devalued.

The concept of god reduces one's world to the unpredictable and incomprehensible. This, of course, is because any form of rational theology, the attempt to prove the existence of god and defend religion, must inevitably collapse to mysticism, usually relying on priests and other agents of the supposedly existent supernatural being to command obedience to the rules of the religion. This is to be accepted on faith, meaning without reason or proof. As Smith says, the concepts of god and religion are decidedly authoritarian.[58]

Religion. To maintain control of followers, priests and the other agents of the supernatural being define and enforce rules of the religion. Nearly all religions worldwide have preached some form of eternal torment for violators, and the torment usually takes place in a location called hell. It is not a pleasant place, so acquiescing to the commands of the god, as dictated by the god's agents, and giving up one's independence is a strongly recommended practice for followers.

The command "'Obey God or burn in hell,'" Smith writes, speaking of the Christian religion, is "a straightforward illustration of a physical sanction, as well as a revealing glimpse into the core of Christianity."[59]

---

[58] Smith, *Atheism*, 297–98.

[59] Smith, *Atheism*, 300.

The threat of physical sanction is what induces fear in followers. Over the centuries Christianity has imposed severe earthly physical sanctions for violation of its rules. Among the most notorious were the torture rack and the stake at which heretics were burned alive, but there were others.

Psychological sanctions, however, have always been more effective. In today's world, Smith points out, "many moderate and liberal denominations [of Christianity] play down the concept of hell or deny it altogether,"[60] and in Western culture the more barbaric physical sanctions have been eliminated. The reason psychological sanctions are more effective is that victims, both children and adults, of physical punishment can and do shrug off the pain as "just physical pain." Mental pain is more serious and controlling because it runs deep; it hurts the core concept of who the person is. It occurs this way because victims internalize the conviction of having done something wrong, having accepted the values and principles of the punisher as morally right and having violated them. Victims of psychological sanctions must agree with their punishers that they are unworthy people by virtue of having committed a sin. Victims of physical sanctions do not necessarily agree with their punishers.

Sin is the concept of choice in many religions to induce guilt, which requires the guilty to ask for forgiveness or redemption, and in turn requires them to feel humility. Guilt is the feeling of having committed a wrong, of having failed to live up to the good, while humility is a sense of unworthiness. An unworthy person is one who is deficient in self-esteem and independence. This, religion requires.

Sin is a thought, desire, or action that disobeys god's will by violating the religion's rules, but it is the thought or desire to transgress that especially induces guilt because religion makes thoughts and desires morally equivalent to actions.

If a man, for example, desires another man's wife, he has according to the Christian religion committed the equivalent of adultery. If such

---

[60] Smith, *Atheism*, 300.

a man, on the other hand, whether religious or not, does not consider it immoral merely to think or to experience her as desirable, he will not feel guilt. The conviction of what constitutes immorality must be present in the man's mind before he will feel guilty for the thought or desire.

Sin, by way of the guilt it causes, says Smith, is Christianity's psychological sanction and is the psychological equivalent of hell. The concept of original sin, allegedly caused by the fall in the Garden of Eden, just magnifies the seriousness and severity of guilt for having sinned; it also makes it impossible for one to be completely moral—we will always be sinners no matter what we do—which further makes independence impossible. "Christianity," says Smith, "thrives on guilt. Guilt, not love, is the fundamental emotion that Christianity seeks to induce. . . . For all of its alleged concern for the 'poor in spirit,' Christianity does its best to perpetuate spiritual impoverishment."[61]

This path to spiritual impoverishment lies in the destruction of self-esteem and independence. A slave, says Smith, cannot "act according to his own judgment," but the Christian God "can monitor, not only the actions of men, but their thoughts and feelings as well. The Christian God can, and does, command how man should think and feel." This, Smith points out, provides a clear connection between religious power and the totalitarian state, for the totalitarian leader, as illustrated throughout much of the twentieth century and acknowledged by observers, aims to "play God."[62]

Indeed, "playing God" is what the social engineers of the Progressives' administrative state were, and still are, doing. There is no omniscient deity in government that can know all the detail and make all the decisions that are required to run, top-down, a modern society, but the Progressives keep trying. Only each individual has the detailed knowledge of what is best for his or her life. No one else has it. This is why a truly free society is "bottom up," in which individuals are free to choose their own values and to act on them

----

[61] Smith, *Atheism*, 304.
[62] Smith, *Atheism*, 306.

without interference from an alleged or pretended omniscient deity, whether god or state.

It is bad enough that the concept of a supernatural being devalues human cognition and therefore self-esteem, the prospect of such a being commanding and controlling one's thoughts and emotions further reduces one's sphere of influence on earth. In fact, it paralyzes thought and feeling, encourages psychological repression, and reduces one to a state of intellectual passivity or what Ayn Rand calls the anticonceptual mentality.[63] It creates abject dependence.[64]

Altruism. From abject dependence, it is a short step to ask for sacrifices. Religious ethics is the doctrine of self-sacrifice known today as altruism.

Self-sacrifice is painful. The word "sacrifice" means "it hurts," and you especially should not get anything in return for the pain. Throwing a child into the fire to pay homage to, or to appease, the gods may be rationalized as giving up a lesser value for the sake of a higher one, and some usage and dictionary definitions of the word "sacrifice" support this notion, but the correct meaning of self-sacrifice in religion and ethics is the act of giving up a higher value to a lower- or non-value. Sacrifice is not a commercial trade in which a buyer gives up money (the lesser value) for a product (the higher value), and vice versa for the seller. Religious and ethical sacrifices are painful and are meant to be painful.[65]

Self-sacrifice means, for example, the pursuit of a career to please one's parents instead of the career one truly loves and wants. It means marrying a person one does not love—again, to please those

---

[63]Smith, *Atheism*, 310. Ayn Rand, "The Missing Link," in *Philosophy: Who Needs It* (Indianapolis: Bobbs-Merrill, 1982), 42–55.

[64]Given the preceding rather dark discussion of gods and religion, let me hasten to add that Christianity's Thomas Aquinas in the thirteenth century revived the thought of Aristotle, paving the way for the seventeenth-century scientific revolution, and the Protestant Reformation, with its emphasis on the ability and desire of each individual Church member to learn to read the Bible and make personal contact with God without the intermediary of priests, enabled the development of individualism, the industrial revolution, and capitalism.

[65]Giving up a higher value for the sake of a lower- or non-value is Ayn Rand's definition of sacrifice. Ayn Rand, "The Ethics of Emergencies," in *The Virtue of Selfishness: A New Concept of Egoism* (New York: New American Library, 1964), 48.

"significant others" who may disapprove of your choice's religion, social class, race, or ethnicity. It means doing your job because it's your duty, not because you enjoy it. It means giving birth to a child you do not want and enslaving yourself to a mistake or accident that occurred when you were young.

In contrast, pursuing the career one desires and enjoys, despite aggravation and opposition from parents; marrying the person one loves, in the face of perceived disappointment and hurt, not to mention possibly vociferous condemnation; and seeking an abortion to terminate a pregnancy and in the process becoming a social outcast—are not sacrifices, provided the choice is a higher value than the one given up.[66]

"Moral purification through suffering" is how the ascetic life is sometimes described. It is the motto of altruism. Immanuel Kant, a devout Protestant, did not know the word "altruism," but he did give us the essence of it: always act from duty, not inclination. Duty, not pleasure or self-interest, is the path to salvation and redemption. This means the most moral persons on earth are ascetics who live the life of sacrifice, even though they, too, while living on earth, are still (original) sinners. All others who do not sacrifice themselves as much as the ascetics are worse sinners. Sacrifice is the only way to assuage one's sins, though we can never fully succeed in doing so, while we are alive on earth.

Autonomy and the pursuit of self-interest, which are required to achieve and maintain self-esteem and independence, are condemned.

The Secular Altruists. It was Auguste Comte who coined the word "altruism," and he meant every bit of the notion of self-sacrifice. For Comte, the golden rule is too selfish, as is Jesus' prescription to love your neighbor as yourself. Suicide is selfish and so are rights.

Writing at libertarianism.org, George Smith quotes Comte's ethics to make clear the meaning of altruism. Comte states that "positivism," Comte's other coined word, which is a broader version of altruism,

---

[66] Spending extra years of one's life, perhaps working at multiple part-time jobs, to acquire an advanced college degree is not, and should not be considered, a sacrifice. Nor should a couple complain about the "sacrifices" they have made to raise a family; they made the choice to have children and presumably value their children more than the childless life they used to enjoy.

never admits anything but duties, of all to all. For its persistently social point of view cannot tolerate the notion of rights, constantly based on individualism. We are born loaded with obligations of every kind, to our predecessors, to our successors, and to our contemporaries. . . . All human rights then are as absurd as they are immoral.[67]

The agnostic Comte developed a secular religion such that our duty, harkening back to the devout Kant, is to all of humanity. As Kant said, our duty is to humanity as an end in itself; humanity is never a means to our own ends. Comte put it this way: "To live for others affords the only means of freely developing the whole existence of man."[68]

Rights, therefore, are out. The collective is in. Does the individual even exist? No, says Comte. "Man . . . as an individual, cannot properly be said to exist, except in the too abstract brain of modern metaphysicians. Existence in the true sense can only be predicated of Humanity."[69]

So sacrifice the individual to the collective. This conforms to the Progressives' theory of the administrative state and the organic theory of society. Altruism and collectivism go together. Ayn Rand was right in her identification that the unprecedented devastation of the twentieth century—between 100 and 300 million war deaths, depending on source—was caused by these two doctrines, for the reason that if someone is preaching the necessity of sacrifice, that someone is most likely collecting the sacrifices. Or, to put it in a colloquial expression, "We were put on earth to serve others, but I don't know why the others were put here." Implied by the expression: we were not put here to develop our independence.[70]

Kindness, gentleness, benevolence, charity—these are not virtues of altruism. Painful self-sacrifice is its essence.

---

[67] Quoted in George H. Smith, "Ayn Rand and Altruism, Part 1," October 23, 2012, https://www.libertarianism.org/publications/essays/excursions/ayn-rand-altruism-part-1.

[68] Quoted in Smith, "Ayn Rand and Altruism."

[69] Quoted in Smith, "Ayn Rand and Altruism."

[70] On war deaths in the twentieth century, see Matthew White, "Necrometrics: Estimated Totals for the Entire 20th Century," last modified September, 2010, http://necrometrics.com/all20c.htm. The political expression of altruism and collectivism is statism. See Ayn Rand, "The Roots of War," in *Capitalism: The Unknown Ideal* (New York: New American Library, 1966), 28–36.

The 1988 book *The Altruistic Personality* by Oliner and Oliner is sometimes taken to present the ideal of altruistic behavior. The book consists of many reflections by rescuers of Jews in Nazi Europe. Fascinating reading, it shows that there were many Anne Franks throughout the occupied countries and several Schindlers. The authors correctly identify Comte as coiner of the word "altruism," meaning duty, selflessness, and not acting on inclination, but then they redefine it for purposes of their study as "rescue behavior," which means anyone who has the courage to act in the face of great risk.

Rescue behavior, however, is an act of courage, not self-sacrifice. Ayn Rand said she would take a bullet for her husband, because her life would not be worth living if she were not able to do everything in her power to save and protect her most cherished value. This does not make Rand an altruist. Nor does the behavior of the Oliners' heroic rescuers of the horrifically scapegoated Jewish victims make them altruists. The rescuers placed a higher value on the decency of human life and the Jewish people's rights than on any risk or danger they may have faced.[71]

Nor is it necessarily altruistic to give money to a friend or relative or to help little old ladies across the street. It depends on one's hierarchy of values: if giving up a higher to a lesser- or non-value is not involved, then the action is not a sacrifice. Gracious generosity may not be a cardinal virtue according to Ayn Rand, but neither is it a vice.

Today, altruism is mostly secular, devoid of religious content. Karl Marx "stood Hegel on his head," removing Hegel's idealism and replacing it with materialism and determinism. He nevertheless retained Hegel's altruism and collectivism. The early Progressives may not have been specifically Marxist in their thinking, but their later representatives, from the 1930s to the present, are decidedly Marxist.

Ever increasing taxes, regulations, and laws in our modern pressure-group-warfare mixed economies are products of the "expert" social engineers of Progressivism. Every new tax, regulation, and law is passed in the name of the "public good" and is an explicit order for

---

[71]Samuel P. Oliner and Pearl M. Oliner, *The Altruistic Personality: Rescuers of Jews in Nazi Europe* (New York: Free Press, 1988).

someone to sacrifice for the sake of that alleged public good. Standing up to and opposing proposals by the "experts" may even lead to investigations by federal prosecutors and threats of criminal charges. In the name of self-sacrifice for the "greater good," modern society continues to move toward total control of every individual. Independence is the enemy of this move.

THE ROOT OF INDEPENDENCE

The above discussions of science and religion, it must be clarified, do not mean that materialists and religious people cannot exhibit independence in areas of their lives. Both Socrates and Galileo were religious and many a materialistic and deterministic scientist, such as Freud, has made remarkably independent discoveries.

The root of independence is fundamentally and primarily psychological. It is not just the ability to pay one's bills. When psychology enters the discussion, we must recognize defense values and the other defensive habits that interfere with effective living.[72] Compartmentalization is one defensive habit that means we can hold different values in different areas of our lives, such as being productive and independent in work but dependent in personal life. This explains how I can praise Socrates and Galileo for their independence and, at the same time, because of compartmentalization, criticize their commitment to religion. The same applies to scientists who espouse materialism and determinism.

My criticism means only that I think the ideas of religion, materialism, and determinism are mistaken and, as a result, harmful to the development of a completely independent life and free society. Independent judgment and action in every area of one's life requires

---

[72] "Defense mechanism" is the more common name of the mental habits we adopt as attempts to fend off anxiety. I prefer to avoid association with Freud's materialism and determinism by replacing "mechanism" with "habit." The concepts of defense values and defensive habits will be developed later in chapter 5. Occasionally, following Edith Packer, I will use "maneuver" instead of "habit." A defensive maneuver, as used here, is a defensive habit, but it also implies or describes a behavioral expression of the habit, such as compulsive handwashing or withdrawal to avoid going out to meet people.

introspective skills to become aware of one's premises, that is, the basic and derivative conscious and subconscious thoughts and values that motivate behavior. To maintain this full independent judgment and action requires the willingness and ability to become aware of mistakes and to correct them.

Independent judgment and action as I am describing it requires responsibility—and effort. To achieve it requires, first, an understanding of the nature of a sound psychological science and the place of independence in that science. It also implies certain requirements for a just and free society. It is to these requirements in chapter 2 that we now turn.

2

Psychology for a Free Society

One of the characteristics of the majority of modern psychological theories, aside from the arbitrariness of so many of their
claims, is their frequently ponderous *irrelevance*. The cause,
both of the irrelevance and of the arbitrariness, is the evident
belief of their exponents that one can have a science of human
nature while consistently ignoring man's most significant and
distinctive attributes.

Psychology, today, is in desperate need of *epistemological*
rehabilitation.

—Nathaniel Branden[1]

PSYCHOLOGY STUDIES AND RECOMMENDS the best use of our
minds—in everyday life, all day, not just occasionally.

Our minds are unique to each of us, so we, as individuals, must
every day choose the correct mental policies to govern our thinking
and thereby guide our choices and actions. Correct thinking, as in all
areas of our lives, but especially in relation to our psychologies, leads
to mentally healthy and happy lives. Incorrect thinking leads to "problems in living," to borrow the phrase from Thomas Szasz.[2]

---

[1]Nathaniel Branden, *The Psychology of Self-Esteem: A Revolutionary Approach to
Self-Understanding that Launched a New Era in Modern Psychology* (San Francisco: Jossey-Bass, 2001), 36 (Branden's italics). First published in 1969 with the
subtitle: *A New Concept of Man's Psychological Nature.*

[2]Szasz, "Myth of Mental Illness." The expression "problems in living" runs throughout the journal article.

Many psychologists and psychiatrists today who are neither Freudians nor behaviorists espouse and practice what is loosely called humanistic psychology. This means they tend to focus on lessening or removing obstacles to each individual's happiness by emphasizing personal growth and fulfillment, sometimes making references to free will or choice. With such emphasis on the individual, one would expect these theoreticians and practitioners to be advocates of capitalism. Most, unfortunately, subscribe to today's disintegrative, epistemological balkanization in which the sciences do not mix: psychology is psychology, so the assumption goes, and politics is politics. The twain do not, and should not, meet.

Some theoreticians and psychiatrists and therapists are explicit advocates of collectivism, despite their psychological emphasis on the individual. Even social psychologists focus on *individuals* in their interactions with others. Very few in the fields of psychology and psychiatry see or acknowledge a connection between psychology and capitalism.[3]

To discuss psychology for a free society and demonstrate the links between the two, we must first establish what a free society is. Then, we can proceed to the nature of psychology and its epistemological foundations, along with a discussion of sound methods of psychological research. This will take us in chapter 3 to the application of the principles of psychology to independence and the significance of independence to capitalism.

THE MEANING OF FREE SOCIETY

A free society is a political association of individuals in which each possesses the identical protection to act without being coerced—by anyone, but especially the government—to work cooperatively via the division of labor to produce prosperity and peace.

---

[3] According to biographer Peter Gay, "Freud was fully persuaded that individual and social psychology are impossible to separate." Peter Gay, *Freud: A Life for Our Time* (New York: W. W. Norton, 1988), 338. On the political spectrum, Freud described himself as a "liberal of the old school," meaning classical liberalism. Quoted in Gay, *Freud*, 16.

Association is entirely voluntary between self-interested consenting adults who exercise their capacity to reason to produce values that are traded with each other to acquire spiritual and material benefits. The result is enhancement—a mutual egoism—of each other's lives. Spiritual benefits include friendship, love, and other non-material values that are not exchanged on the market for money. Material benefits, however, most often are so exchanged; they include the production of wealth through the creation of capital goods, which in turn create consumer goods. A rapidly rising standard of living is consequence of this voluntary and self-interested consent.

The free society is a liberal society. The term used here refers to the institution of classical liberalism, the product of Enlightenment values and benefactor of human life over the past two hundred years that has brought humankind out of abject poverty to a life of luxury unimaginable in earlier years.

The free society is a social system called laissez-faire capitalism. It is not just an economic system, as capitalism is based on individual rights, those freedoms of action that are required for survival and comfort. Rights derive from and are inherent in the nature of humans as rational beings. Freedom of action means, in Ayn Rand's clarifying formulation, no one may *initiate* physical force against anyone else; everyone receives identical protection from such initiated coercion and is therefore equal before the law. Freedom of action, finally, means the right, through trade, to acquire, use, and dispose of property as one sees fit. Property rights are the implementation of the rights to life and liberty and constitute the foundation without which a free society cannot flourish.[4]

Rights, freedom, equality, and property—these are the essential concepts.

The free society more fundamentally rests on a theory of human nature that acknowledges the supremacy of reason to know reality and to guide our actions. It assumes that as beings who possess the capacity

---

[4] Ayn Rand, "Man's Rights," in *Virtue of Selfishness*, 122–34. Rand, "What Is Capitalism?" in *Capitalism: The Unknown Ideal*, 3–27.

to reason, we must each independently exercise that capacity to produce and acquire values for our own self-interested gain. All physically
healthy adults who possess normal brains are capable of making this
choice and are therefore capable of supporting themselves. Those who
do not make the choice are consenting to become dependent on others to provide for them.

Errors made during the Enlightenment failed to give reason, egoism, and individualism their full due, thus allowing ancient hostilities
to self-responsibility to emerge and intensify under the new banner
of statism, by demanding obedience to the authority of a collective
or the state instead of to a god or gods. The theory of human nature
that reason is limited and incapable of perceiving reality correctly, or
directly, and therefore cannot guide actions in a reliable way, means
that humans cannot be independent or self-responsible. They must be
provided for, led, and coerced by an elite who knows what is best. The
Hobbesian Leviathans, or rather, omnipotent governments, of the twentieth and twenty-first centuries were the result. Enlightenment errors
allowed religious virtue to become secularized as political and psychological dependence. Socialism became the social system of choice
to modernize, and rationalize, self-sacrifice and coercion as a way of
life. Government became our god and we must now bow down to it as
our master and friend.[5]

---

[5]Statism is the broader concept that subsumes communism and socialism, on the
one hand, and fascism, on the other. In the former the state abolishes all private
property, while in the latter it controls and regulates what is private property
in name only. In all cases, the individual must sacrifice his or her welfare to
the state, thus producing a totalitarian society. The need for an elite to rule is
rationalized by assuming the masses are ignorant, unintelligent, and lack good
judgment. The elite in our post-Enlightenment world are the PhD-Kings of a
bureaucracy (or "deep state") that maintains and exercises exclusive control over
the initiation of the use of physical force. As recent history has demonstrated,
the legalized monopoly on initiated coercion has enabled the more ruthless to
rise to the top. Hence, the last one hundred years of beyond-savage, terroris-
tic dictatorships. On the identification of fascism as "socialism of the German
pattern," see Ludwig von Mises, *Human Action: A Treatise on Economics*, 3d rev.
ed. (Chicago: Henry Regnery, 1966), 716–19, 758–79, 858–61 First edition published in German in 1940. George Reisman, *Capitalism: A Treatise on Economics*
(Laguna Hills, CA: TJS Books, 1996), 263–64. On why the worst rise to the top,
see F. A. Hayek, *The Road to Serfdom: A Classic Warning Against the Dangers to*

Historically, freedom meant, and today still means, capable of acting without being controlled by others, especially church, king, or state. In history, one of the ironically sad problems classical liberals faced when arguing for a free society was that many serfs and slaves resisted being freed. They feared how they would take care of themselves and many apologists for the authoritarian state, because of their theory of human nature, agreed that serfs and slaves were incapable of independence.[6] In the era of the Soviet Union, there were stories of Russian citizens who were allowed to leave for a visit to the West but chose to return, because the totalitarian paradise of communism felt safer than freedom. The same can be said about many victims of controlling and abusive personal relationships; aside from fear of reprisal for walking away, many of these victims simply do not have the strength to leave.

The strength I am talking about is psychological. The essential requirement for a free society is a strong personal identity manifested as a high level of self-esteem. This brings us to our main discussion, the relationship between psychology and freedom.

THE SCIENCE OF MENTAL PROCESSES

The underlying premise of this work is that unobstructed mental functioning—an uninhibited psychology—requires unobstructed, uninhibited, physical functioning within the social world. This means an unhampered consciousness and an unhampered market—the free society—go together. The one requires and reinforces the other.

The Human Being's Capacity to Reason

Psychology as a science studies the nature and functions of consciousness, whether human or not. The essential distinguishing characteristic of human beings is the capacity to reason, the ability

Freedom Inherent in Social Planning (Chicago, University of Chicago Press, 1944), chap. 10. The legalization of initiated coercion attracts those willing to use it, and those most willing to use coercion advance faster than those who are hesitant.

[6]Ludwig von Mises, *Liberalism in the Classical Tradition*, trans. Ralph Raico (William Volker Fund, 1962; repr., San Francisco: Cobden Press, 1985), 20–23. First published in German in 1927.

through conceptualization to generate and direct action to the achievement of chosen goals. To survive and flourish, humans require general knowledge, or education, in the form of concepts and principles to guide their choices and actions. Each individual, in addition, requires specific knowledge, or a set of concepts and principles unique to his or her experience, to direct action to the achievement of health and happiness.

Thus, psychology as it applies to human beings studies the nature and functions of a rational consciousness. This is a consciousness that must choose to exercise its capacity to reason, to direct perception to relevant areas of its environment, then to identify and integrate the facts of reality.[7] Identification means forming the concepts and principles that constitute one's general and specific knowledge; integration, guided by logic, ensures that accumulated knowledge is consistent within itself and, more importantly, tied to the facts, that is, not "floating."[8]

All of this activity of consciousness is volitional, which means we are free to choose any part of it, or none of it. We are free to perform the functions of our rational consciousness in a precise and accurate

[7] This is a paraphrase of Ayn Rand's definition of reason. Ayn Rand, "The Objectivist Ethics," in *Virtue of Selfishness*, 13.

[8] A floating abstraction is a concept, principle, or theory not connected, directly or indirectly, to the facts of reality it claims to represent. The notion "floats" in the air, as it were, or away from shore—land or the shore being reality. It may sound impressive, but when analyzed it turns out to be fluff. It may consist of definitions by non-essentials, lacking clear genus or differentia; excessive and unnecessary detail, often vague or ambiguous; emotional associations (connotation) of the speaker or writer unrelated to the meaning or referents of the abstraction (denotation); or just plain falsehoods. Ayn Rand, *Introduction to Objectivist Epistemology*, expanded 2nd ed. (New York: NAL Books, 1990), 42–43. First book edition published by Mentor in 1979. Core chapters 1–8 originally published in *The Objectivist*, July 1966–February 1967. Barbara Branden, "Efficient Thinking," guest lecture in Nathaniel Branden, *The Vision of Ayn Rand: The Basic Principles of Objectivism* (Gilbert, AZ: Cobden Press, 2009), 178–79. Transcription of twenty-lecture series offered between 1958 and 1968. Barbara Branden, *Think As If Your Life Depends On It: Principles of Efficient Thinking & Other Lectures* (Published by the author's estate, CreateSpace, 2017), 113–21. Chapters 1–10 a transcription of ten-lecture series offered in the early 1960s. For Rand, truth is not a correspondence theory, as in mirroring or reflecting the facts of reality. It is a "recognition" or "identification" theory, because consciousness is an active process of differentiation and integration in the determination of truth. "Truth is the product of the recognition (i.e., identification) of the facts of reality." Rand, *Objectivist Epistemology*, 48, 5.

manner that yields knowledge in our minds—beliefs and values that correctly identify reality. Or, we can refuse to perform any functions at all, relying on others to do the mental work. Or, we can perform in varying degrees of accuracy and completeness, such as thinking precisely in some areas and not at all in others, or thinking in a disordered, half-hearted manner in all areas. This range of how we can use our minds contributes to the wide variation in personalities we all exhibit.

Some of the failures to perform the rational functions of consciousness can be deliberate and willful, as in the case of a criminal personality that revels in lying to and cheating others and, generally, getting away with the forbidden. Other failures can result from psychological inhibitions, such as defense values and the other defensive habits that, to be sure, are created by us, but in the present we often do not experience as in our control. We may not even be aware of them.

Or, we may just be ignorant—having never been taught, which includes nearly all of us—of how to perform the functions required by our rational consciousness. Poor learning about how to use our minds causes us to be buffeted by environmental influences, whether parental, educational, or cultural. We all still have free will, of course, so some of us will choose better ways of handling the influences than others. Those who choose not to think at all, or to think in a less than honest way, will likely decide to follow the path of the criminal; most of us choose some kind of coping habits and become inhibited in our psychological functioning. Some degree of dependence and unhappiness is the result.

It is in this way that our character and personality are self-created. Character defines who we are as a moral person and consists of our beliefs and values about what is required to flourish as a being that possesses the capacity to reason. This includes the identification and acceptance of such moral values as honesty, integrity, and courage. Personality, the broader term, is our distinctive method of thinking and acting; it includes all of our beliefs and values—the moral ones, as well as the ones that form our psychologies, that is, beliefs and values about who we are as a person, beliefs and values about other people, and beliefs and values about the environment in which we live. The outward behavioral manifestation of beliefs and values are called traits and the traits that stand out, the distinctive ones, define our personality.

From the time we begin to talk, as toddlers, which is the time we begin to form concepts and, soon after, elementary principles, right up to the present, we have drawn innumerable conclusions—a myriad of thoughts—about all kinds of things, and any one of them may have been logical or illogical, correct or incorrect. These thousands of conclusions accumulate and become the mental habits by which we live our lives. As habits, especially in adulthood, many have become so automatized, buried in our subconscious with their origins largely forgotten, that they *feel* to us as if we were born that way, or that something external is making us act the way we do.

The Genes-Environment Debate

This brings us to the genes versus environment, or nature versus nurture, debate that dominates thinking in psychology today. But neither genes nor environment cause behavior.

If genes caused behavior, one would expect to see evidence in infants of criminality, genius, schizophrenia, homosexuality, and evangelical Christianity. All of these behaviors, plus many others, have been said to be inborn. To expect an infant to exhibit these traits is absurd. To say that an infant has inherited the *potential* to become a criminal, or evangelical Christian, says nothing and explains nothing. We are all born with that potential, plus countless other potentialities.

The trouble with environment as a cause of behavior is that there are always exceptions to the good and bad things environment does to children. Some children reared in crime-ridden, slum neighborhoods become criminals while others do not, even if they are siblings in the same family. The same can be said for children reared in safe, wealthy suburbs. Others raised in evangelical Christian families follow their parents and become religious, while some rebel and become atheists.

The Twin Studies. Consider the twin studies that allegedly demonstrate genetic and biological determinism of our behavior. For nearly a hundred years the twin studies have attempted to prove that many of our traits are inherited. Psychologist Jay Joseph has thoroughly examined the studies of identical and fraternal twins, both reared together and reared apart, and has declared them "one of the great pseudo-scientific methods of our time . . . [that] will eventually be added to the list of discarded pseudosciences where we now find alchemy, craniometry, and mesmerism."[9]

The fundamental problem with the twin studies, contrary to their claims, is that they cannot hold constant the potentially confounding environment. Identical and same-sex fraternal twins reared together are assumed to experience identical, or very nearly identical, environments. This alleged identical environment means that any greater behavioral similarity between identical, as opposed to fraternal, twins is due to genetic inheritance. However, identical twins experience a more similar environment than do their same-sex fraternal counterparts. And this has been acknowledged by most twin researchers since the 1960s. Their studies, as Joseph concludes, merely point out that identical twins are given "more similar treatment" and therefore experience "greater environmental similarity."[10] With the rising interest and research in epigenetics, even the assumption of a 100% match in genetic profile of identical twins has been questioned.[11]

---

[9] Jay Joseph, "Has a New Twin Study Meta-Analysis Finally 'Settled' the Nature-Nurture Debate?," *Mad in America: Science, Psychiatry and Social Justice* (blog), June 1, 2015, https://www.madinamerica.com/category/blogs/. Search blog title. See also Joseph, *The Gene Illusion: Genetic Research in Psychiatry and Psychology Under the Microscope* (New York: Algora Publishing, 2004). Joseph, *The Trouble with Twin Studies: A Reassessment of Twin Research in the Social and Behavioral Sciences* (New York: Routledge, 2015).

[10] Joseph, "The Trouble with Twin Studies," *Mad in America: Science, Psychiatry and Social Justice* (blog), March 13, 2013, https://www.madinamerica.com/category/blogs/. Search blog title. Joseph, *The Gene Illusion*, chap. 2.

[11] Joseph, *Trouble with Twin Studies* (book), 99–100. Eye color is a nearly 100% match (concordance) between identical twins. The many personality and behavioral traits that are said to be genetic do not come close to such a rate. Nor do some physical diseases. Lung and skin cancer, for example, have a nearly zero concordance. N. E. and B. K. Whitehead, *My Genes Made Me Do It*, 5th ed., (n.p.: Whitehead Associates, 2018), 176. Available for download at http://www.mygenes.co.nz. First edition published in 1999.

Rather than reject the twin method, some researchers accept the above points and then engage in circular reasoning, by assuming as true what is stated in a premise to prove the same thing in the conclusion. They admit that identical twins "create" or "elicit" similar environments to each other, but claim, in Joseph's words, that this is only "because they are more similar genetically."[12] Citing a proponent of this theory, Joseph quotes Nancy Segal in her 2012 book *Born Together—Reared Apart* as, first, stating the premise of the circular reasoning that "shared genes underlie similarity between relatives," then later in the book, the conclusion "that personality similarity between relatives seems to come mostly from their shared genes."[13]

Studies of identical twins reared apart do not help. As Joseph and other critics have thoroughly analyzed, the studies commit hosts of methodological errors. The samples, for one, are small and there are few of them. Almost none of the twins have been separated from each other at birth; one pair lived together until age nine before being separated and another lived next door to each other. The subjects in one study were given all-expense-paid trips to the research location in order to be interviewed, demonstrably biasing their responses to interview questions. The researchers in their reports emphasized similarities between the twins—similarities, as Joseph points out, that could have occurred naturally due to age and culture—and ignored differences. And the researchers of the last significant study of twins reared apart have refused to make their data available to independent analysts.[14]

---

[12]Joseph, *Trouble with Twin Studies* (book), 158.

[13]Quoted in Joseph, *Trouble with Twin Studies* (book), 114.

[14]Joseph, "'Bewitching Science' Revisited: Tales of Reunited Twins and the Genetics of Behavior," *Mad in America: Science, Psychiatry and Social Justice* (blog), March 6, 2016, https://www.madinamerica.com/category/blogs/. Search blog title. The popular press has uncritically propagandized the findings of many twin studies and treated researchers as celebrities of science. One "celebrity" researcher (Segal), referring to two identical males reared apart, cited as evidence of genetic influence their habit of curling the pinkie finger under a beer can. This was cited in books published in 1999 and then again in 2012, despite the criticism in intervening years that many non-twins exhibit the same habit and that there are only three ways to hold such a can. Joseph, *Trouble with Twin Studies* (book), 121–22. That last significant twin study was funded in large part

The Criminal Personality. Now consider the criminal personality that is usually, though not always, said to be determined by unpleasant environments, such as slum neighborhoods and alcoholic, drug addicted, or imprisoned parents. Psychologist Stanton Samenow disagrees.[15]

For over forty years, Samenow has been interviewing criminal offenders. His conclusion is that criminals are not criminals because of their upbringing or environment, or because of what they see on television or in movies. Criminals are who they are because of the thoughts they hold, and have held, in their minds from an early age.[16]

When many people walk into a crowded room, they think about who they would enjoy talking to. The criminal first checks escape routes, then looks for items to steal or weak targets to intimidate, manipulate, swindle, or rob. Criminals go to great lengths, sometimes using a considerable intelligence, to plan their crimes.

The criminal mind enjoys, or gets a jolt of excitement, as Samenow puts it, by doing what is wrong and getting away with it. "If rape were legalized today," said one offender, "I wouldn't rape. I would

by the Pioneer Fund, founded in 1937 to research race science and eugenics. The researchers insist there was no connection to eugenics in their project or pressure from the fund. Joseph discusses the issues here: Joseph, *Trouble with Twin Studies* (book), 253–58. In his latest book, *Schizophrenia and Genetics: The End of an Illusion* (self-pub., Amazon Digital Services, 2017), Kindle, Joseph continues his campaign against genetic determinism.

[15] Criminality, of course, is often said to be genetically or biologically determined, but criticisms of the twin studies above also apply here. As does the classic critique of any kind of human or animal behavior allegedly caused by instincts: Daniel S. Lehrman, "A Critique of Konrad Lorenz's Theory of Instinctive Behavior," *The Quarterly Review of Biology* 28, no. 4 (December 1953): 337–63.

[16] The pioneer in this field was Samuel Yochelson who was also Samenow's mentor. The two wrote a three-volume work *The Criminal Personality*. Most important for consideration here are volumes one and two, *A Profile for Change* (1976; repr., Northvale, NJ: Jason Aronson, 1993), and *The Change Process* (1977; repr., Northvale, NJ: Jason Aronson, 1994). Samenow's subsequent works include *Inside the Criminal Mind*, rev. ed. (1984; repr., New York: Broadway Books, 2014), *Before It's Too Late: Why Some Kids Get into Trouble—and What Parents Can Do About It* (New York: Crown Books, 1989; New York: Three Rivers Press, 2001), and *The Myth of the "Out of Character" Crime* (Westport, CT: Praeger, 2007; self-pub., CreateSpace, 2010).

do something else." The criminal act has to be illegal, otherwise the criminal would not experience the excitement.[17]

When criminals get caught, they blame themselves only for being stupid and careless. When interviewed by the courts and Samenow, they either never admit to their wrongdoing or blame their behavior on external circumstances, such as upbringing or environment. They insist that they are good human beings and find no contradiction to "pray at ten o'clock [and] rob at noon."[18] Some even express disgust at child abusers, then rob and murder someone who, according to their way of thinking, "deserved it."

Samenow repeatedly insists, demonstrating with many examples, that not all criminals suffer family abuse or undesirable surroundings. Criminals come from all walks of life and include the highly educated and intelligent. They all have siblings and other relatives who grow up in the same family cultures and environmental conditions and do not turn out the way they did.

What criminals have in common is lying as a way of life, and it starts young. A child of five or six may lift a friend's or sibling's toy and get a thrill out of it. Denying guilt or blaming someone else—and getting away with the theft—provides another thrill and encourages further, more daring behavior.

People who follow the rules, according to such a young child (or adult) thief, are suckers. Their lives are boring. "My life of crime," thinks the criminal, "is exciting." It is these thoughts that drive the criminal mind to plan the next "exciting" caper.

Criminals do not have friends, because they trust no one; they see other people as targets to manipulate. They do nonetheless gravitate to each other so they can share illegal adventures and plan bigger and bigger payoffs. They have nothing in common with the child or adult who lives a responsible, law-abiding life. Criminals envy the nice things in life, such as a home, car, or expensive

---

[17] Samenow, *Out of Character*, 12.

[18] Stanton E. Samenow, "Pray at Ten O'Clock, Rob at Noon," *Concept of the Month—March 2014* (blog), http://www.samenow.com/conceptmarch_14.html.

computer, but they cannot conceive of working to attain these values. They would rather take them.

Can criminals change? Not easily. Those who try to settle down in a job to make money for a car or home often succumb to their urges for the excitement of crime. Samenow does relate one success story of an armed robber and home invader who changed, but he had to go through a long process of catching his criminal thoughts midstream, challenging them, and struggling to substitute better ones. The process required is not unlike the will power of recovering alcoholics who must repeatedly check their desires for a drink.[19]

In addition to dispelling the myth of environmental determinism as cause of criminal behavior, Samenow demonstrates that there is no such thing as a "crime of passion," the so-called out-of-character crime. The reason, again, is the thoughts the criminal holds. A sudden and gruesome knifing, Samenow reveals, is not so surprising and out of character when one discovers the hostile thoughts, resentments, and fantasies of stabbing or killing the target that the criminal has experienced for many months or years.[20]

Samenow concludes, "I have found that thinking errors are causal in every case of criminal conduct. . . .The *error* is a flaw in the thought process that results in behavior that injures others. The harm done may be minor or extremely serious."[21]

The Cause of Behavior

The genes-environment axis is so steeped in determinism that each side flails away at the other claiming their side effectively does away with that thing called consciousness and its alleged free will. The determinism of the genes-environment axis, however, is a self-contradiction. Its proponents pretend to be making a logical choice to believe

---

[19] Samenow, *Inside the Criminal Mind*, chap. 15.

[20] Samenow, *Out of Character*, throughout. "The theme of this book is that *people always respond in character*. . . . The 'out of character' crime can be understood only by figuring out what the character of the alleged perpetrator truly is" (Samenow's italics). Samenow, *Out of Character*, 1.

[21] Samenow, *Out of Character*, 6–7 (Samenow's italics).

in determinism, yet they have to acknowledge that they are determined to believe in determinism. That means something other than genes or environment must be operating to cause our behavior.

The Primacy of Thought. And that something is our thought, or lack of it. More precisely, good thought causes good behavior; bad thought, or the lack of thought, causes bad behavior. Thinking errors, to generalize Samenow's observations about criminals, are causal not just in producing criminals, but in producing psychological problems and unhappiness in responsible citizens. Thinking accuracy produces mental health and happiness. Thinking accuracy in all areas of our lives is the cause of independence and independent judgment.

Thought is what processes our genetic inheritance and environment. One genetic inheritance relevant for this discussion, and requiring significant thought, is our needs, because that is where motivation and behavior begin.

All living species have needs, that is, specific requirements for their survival and well-being. Without necessarily endorsing Abraham Maslow's hierarchy of needs, or offering the following as exhaustive, humans possess physiological and psychological needs that must be satisfied throughout our lives, though the specific manifestations in which we satisfy the needs may vary with age, development, and choice.[22] As long as we are alive, we need food, shelter, and clothing. In infancy and childhood (and adulthood), we need warmth, love, nurturance, and education—especially education in how to use our minds. Our essential psychological need is for self-esteem, which in adulthood is primarily pursued and sustained through a productive career.[23] Our most fundamental need is to exercise our capacity to reason.

Failure to satisfy a need constitutes a deficiency that must be remedied by acting to acquire a value. Hunger, for example, is a sign that

---

[22] Abraham Maslow, "A Theory of Human Motivation," *Psychological Review* 50, no. 4 (1943): 370–96, https://dx.doi.org/10.1037/h0054346. For another view of needs, cf. Glasser, *Choice Theory*, chap. 2.

[23] The following rests heavily on Branden, *Psychology of Self-Esteem*, chap. 2 and throughout. I am not ruling out parenting, at least for a part of our lives, as productive.

our physiological need for food is not being met. Hence, we are motivated to look for the remedy. Mistakes, however, can be made and we may get sick by eating the wrong thing. Similarly, obsessive anxiety is a sign that our psychological need for self-esteem is not being satisfied, so we search for solutions to the fear that seems to have no cause. If we fail to deal with the anxiety directly and remove it with better mental policies, we may choose defense values and other defensive habits as a salve for the anxiety. Such salves, though, do not work and we will suffer problems in living that constrict our lives and happiness.

Needs are the starting point of motivation and behavior, but we are the ones who must choose to think about them. We must identify what our needs are and what will satisfy them. Or to put it more precisely, someone must think about those needs. If we don't, then our parents and teachers must. Young children rely on their elders to teach them, but we all still have the choice to accept or reject what has been taught us—if not when young, then at a later age.

The conclusions we draw about needs constitute our beliefs about what we think is true. Beliefs may be true or false, depending in part on how well (completely and accurately) we have monitored our thinking about those needs and in part on how good (complete and true) our available knowledge is. Faulty past thinking, as well as ignorance, can cause us to form false beliefs.

In addition to true or false beliefs, conclusions also include evaluations that may be true or false—true in the sense of being factually beneficial to us or false in the sense of being harmful. Evaluations, or more simply, values, produce emotions that carry with them a tendency to act.[24] Emotions are automatic, psychosomatic responses to evaluations of what we believe to be beneficial or harmful. Emotions that humans can experience range from the broad to the subtle, as well as most significantly from the pleasant to the unpleasant. If pleasant,

---

[24]Evaluation is the process. Value is the product, the result of an evaluation. Both are mental. There is no *intrinsic* value, "out there, in the thing," but neither are our values subjective if they are chosen based on an objective standard of what is beneficial or harmful to us. Rand, "What Is Capitalism?" 14–15.

the tendency to act will be to approach, acquire, and enjoy the value; if unpleasant, the tendency will be to avoid, destroy, or forget. This process indicates that emotions have causes and that they are changeable, but only by changing the beliefs and evaluations that cause them.

Behavior results from our choice to act on one of these tendencies, though we do not have to make that choice. We may choose some other tendency to act, or choose not to act at all.

This is the essence of human motivation—and free will.

To illustrate the process in a highly simplified manner, a boy believes he has a need for a productive career, because he has been taught it from an early age. He accepts the notion as a healthy belief, evaluates it favorably, and experiences the emotional desire to work hard and to go to college to pursue his career. He so chooses to act on the desire. Consequently, in adulthood he feels like an accomplished person.

A girl, on the other hand, is taught that her need is to serve others, especially to sacrifice herself to her husband and family. She chooses to accept this as a belief and evaluates it favorably (and may even evaluate the thought of pursuing a career negatively, even though at an earlier age she may have had a desire to pursue a career, but gave it up). She feels the strong desire to focus her attention on attracting boys, to skip college to get married and have a large family. She so chooses this path. Later in life, she feels unfulfilled as a woman, experiences anxiety and depression, and must seek help from a psychotherapist.[25]

Thought, including faulty thought, combined with our accumulated knowledge, both accurate and faulty, generate motivation and direct behavior. Consciousness, more broadly and significantly, is what regulates our actions, but it is a rational consciousness that is volitional, which means we can commit errors, willfully or accidentally, anywhere in the process. Thinking errors are the main cause of false beliefs and false values. The formation of false beliefs and false values are what

---

[25]The examples, again, are highly simplified, as psychologies are much more complicated. The assumption of both is that boys and girls have a psychological need for a productive career. The example of the girl is "the problem that has no name" from Betty Friedan, *The Feminine Mystique* (New York: W. W. Norton, 1963), chap. 1.

leads to behaviors harmful to ourselves, and, if other people are involved in the values, to them as well. False beliefs and values are the source of psychological problems and criminal personalities. Happiness and success in life require the opposite, correct beliefs and correct values. If not happy or successful, adjustment of the false beliefs and values will be required.

As a being who possesses the capacity to reason, we must scrutinize our reasoning in order not to make mistakes. Free will is cognitive self-regulation, which means we may choose to focus on the facts or evade them, allowing other factors, such as emotions, presuppositions, ignorance, or political doctrine, to interfere with correct perception. Free will is the choice to think or not to think, and we are the controller of those thought processes. No one else is.

The unfortunate consequence of the genes-environment debate is that the axis devalues, or does not even consider, the environmental influence of an education in sound psychology. For that is what is required to help us use our free will to properly assess genetic inheritance and environment and thereby make better choices to live a happier life.

The Mental Habits by Which We Live. Our guide to the correct perception of reality is that 2400-year-old science of thinking called logic, Aristotelian logic. As the discipline and art that regulates internal thought processes, logic is *the* introspective science. The genes-environment axis, however, does not want to admit that logic is introspective, because then its advocates would have to admit that consciousness controls behavior and that introspection is a valid method of science.

From the practical perspective, mental habits formed from the time we are young influence our present behavior. Mental habits are distinctive ways in which we use our minds, that is, process the data of reality to guide our choices and actions. The distinctive ways of using our minds technically are called psycho-epistemologies, but they can also be thought of as distinctive psychological traits that define our personality.[26] As

---

[26] Ayn Rand, *For the New Intellectual* (New York: Signet, 1961), 21. Branden, *Psychology of Self-Esteem*, 96–98. Barbara Branden, *Think As If Your Life Depends on*

habits, of course, they can be good or bad, based on true or false thoughts or true or false evaluations, or both, which generate emotions that can conflict with other emotions, which means other true or false thoughts or evaluations. Some of the thoughts and evaluations may be subconscious, leaving us little awareness of what is going on.

All thoughts, evaluations, and emotions can be changed, though not always easily; habits, after all, are learned. Just as we were not born knowing how to drive a car, we were not born depressed or angry or schizophrenic.[27]

A depressed person, for example, who has just been fired may evaluate the situation and conclude, "I'll never find another job," or who has just been jilted may conclude, "I'll never find another lover." These thoughts are false, as logic applied to their thinking finds no objective threat to their ability to find new employment, or to find new romantic partners. Hidden, possibly subconscious premises are also likely operating in these cases, such as, "Only losers get fired or jilted. I'm no good. No one will ever want to hire me or love me." These depressed people must identify and change their conscious and subconscious premises to something more accurate about their situations. Not until then will they begin to feel better. It is in this way that thinking errors lead to unhappiness. These unhappy people may need professional help, or a perceptive and empathic friend.

Indeed, the thinking of these people can be expressed as a logical syllogism. "Anyone who gets fired or jilted is a loser. I got fired-jilted. Therefore, I am a loser." The focus of therapist or friend in helping

---

It, chap. 1 and throughout. Barbara Branden is credited with alerting both Ayn Rand and Nathaniel Branden to the importance of this subject. Branden, *Psychology of Self-Esteem*, 277n1 (chap. 6). Cf. Rudolf Dreikurs, "The Private Logic" in Harold H. Mosak, ed., *Alfred Adler: His Influence on Psychology Today* (Park Ridge, NJ: Noyes Press, 1973), 19–32. "Private logic" and similar terms were used initially by Alfred Adler to indicate neurotic reasoning, but followers, including Dreikurs, broadened it to cover thinking patterns of both normal and abnormal psychologies.

[27] "Mental" is redundant when talking about habits, as they are all formed and automatized through conscious practice. Psycho-epistemologies, as discussed here, are habitual ways of using and regulating consciousness.

unhappy people, however, is not on analyzing, textbook style, the logical structure of their thinking, but on the falseness of the first premise and conclusion. The premise and conclusion are what need to be challenged and changed; a lecture or sermon on Logic 101 is not what is called for. Logical analysis of one's psychology is about consistency between all of our thoughts and their correct identification of the facts of reality.

Certain habits, generated from what psychologist Edith Packer calls core evaluations, plus other less fundamental but nevertheless significant evaluations, are usually acquired when young, from toddlerhood on. In particular, we subconsciously make and retain early conclusions in three influential areas: ourselves, other people, and the world in general (reality). All three, but especially the first one, produce our sense of personal identity. Core evaluations are held in our minds as unquestioned absolutes. They have become automatized habits that "operate without our permission," as Packer puts it, to influence our development and present actions.[28]

In toddlerhood, when we begin to speak, we are beginning to think in concepts and words, but young children do not usually form important conclusions through explicit reasoning. They often do it through a process of emotional generalization and often, though not always,

---

[28] Packer, "Understanding the Subconscious" in *Lectures on Psychology: A Guide to Understanding Your Emotions* (Laguna Hills, CA: TJS Books, 2018), 7. *Lectures on Psychology* was first published in 2012 as a Kindle e-book. Packer's work thus falls into the cognitive tradition of psychology. However, cognitive psychology is imbued with a form of behavioral determinism, so critical reading is required. Cf. Aaron Beck, "Thinking and Depression," *Archives of General Psychiatry* 9, no. 10 (October 1963): 324–33; Aaron Beck, "Thinking and Depression II: Theory and Therapy," *Archives of General Psychiatry* 10, no. 6 (June 1964): 561–71; and Judith S. Beck, *Cognitive Behavior Therapy: Basics and Beyond*, 2nd ed., (New York: Guilford Press, 2011), 30–36. First edition published in 1995. Aaron Beck's conception of an "automatic thought" mistakenly conflates the three components of a cognition: our belief about what is true, our evaluative judgment of what is beneficial or harmful, and our emotional reaction to some object, person, or event. Only emotional reactions are truly automatic; beliefs and evaluations are programmed and automatized, that is, made habitual, by us. Judith Beck's "core beliefs" about self, others, and the world is a better concept but she still uses her father's automatic thoughts and does not focus solely or clearly on the evaluative judgment. Both use Kant's confusing concept, filtered by Piaget, of the "schema." Neither refers to the subconscious.

through imitation of or absorption from the behavior of their parents. At the risk of oversimplification, an emotion at this stage in life, if it could be put into words, might say something like, "That made me feel good about myself. I'll do it again." Or, "I didn't like that, so I'm not going to feel it next time."[29]

Core evaluations that can result from these generalizations, on the positive side, using Packer's examples, might be: "Values are achievable and happiness is possible." Or, "Life is an adventure." On the negative side, core evaluations might be: "Life is a power struggle and, being weak, I will always be defeated." Or, "The real me is bad."[30]

Repeated many times, the former emotional generalization and resulting positive core evaluations, because they are based on a correct perception of reality, can lead to the development of self-esteem and the potential for and eventual accomplishment of happiness. The latter generalization and negative core evaluations, which are mistaken, can lead to repression and subsequent psychological problems, plus the likelihood of unhappiness. And a child can form and hold both positive and negative core evaluations at the same time, which means internal conflict later in life, the development of defensive maneuvers to attempt to deal with the anxiety produced by the conflict, and a less than independent and happy psychology.

It is through this process of the early formation of mistaken core evaluations, and other thinking errors, that the development of independence and independent judgment becomes dampened and possibly prevented from developing at all. If we are taught from an early age,

---

[29] The root and cause of early emotional generalizations, probably since birth but certainly in infancy, is our inborn ability to experience pleasure and pain. An infant, for example, who is hit and abused will form negative generalizations and emotions about self and others, due to treatment of the caregiver. Later emotional generalizations, when the child is older and has learned to speak, are still guided by our sensitivity to pleasure and pain, but the generalizations need to be conceptualized. The child's failure to conceptualize results from its failure to introspect, which, in today's culture, means the failure of parents and teachers to teach the child introspective skill. Without introspection at an early age, chance emotional generalization becomes our subconscious driver.

[30] Packer, "Understanding the Subconscious," 4.

however, to look inward to identify our beliefs, evaluations, and emotions, especially our core evaluations, and to correct errors we have made, we would mature with healthy psychologies.

Most of us have not been taught much of anything about psychology, in childhood or adulthood. Thus, when the genes-environment axis comes along, it seems to make sense that our behavior is caused by something we have no control over. The irony is that genes and environment do influence us, in the sense that genes give us needs, gender, height, and hair color, and environment can make our lives easy or difficult, but we are the ones who develop attitudes about gender, height, environment, and, most importantly, what our needs are and what can satisfy them.

To help us correctly perceive and evaluate what genetics has given us and what goes on in our environment, teaching is crucial. Parents and the schools need to instruct children in the skill of introspection, the skill of applying logic to their own psychologies.

THE INDIVIDUALISM OF PSYCHOLOGY

In a May 1973 interview in *Reason* magazine, Nathaniel Branden was asked about the connection between his psychological theories and his political convictions. His answer was that psychology and politics both rest on a theory of human nature and that if a psychologist teaches autonomy and self-responsibility both in the classroom and therapist's office, but in political life preaches collectivism and statism, that psychologist must eventually confront, as Branden put it, a "radical contradiction." He emphasized that it is the humanistic psychologists of Abraham Maslow's "third force" (psychoanalysis and behaviorism being the other two forces) that should most conspicuously experience this contradiction. Sooner or later, Branden said, "the contradiction will explode in their faces."[31]

---

[31] On Maslow's third force, see Abraham Maslow, *Toward a Psychology of Being* (Blacksburg, VA: Wilder Publications, 2011), 8. First published in 1962. The interview of Branden was reprinted in Nathaniel Branden, *The Disowned Self* (New York: Bantam Books, 1973), 141–67. Besides Branden, Thomas Szasz, Peter Breggin, and Edith Packer acknowledge the connection between psychology and

Alas, as of now this explosion does not seem to have occurred.[32] Yet psychology is about as individualistic a science as one can get. There is no collective consciousness (or brain). The words "society" and "social," in any proper understanding of the concepts, can only refer to the sum of their individual constituents. And "psychobabble" is not an inappropriate word to use to describe the preaching of those who claim that the "whole (of society) is greater than the sum of its parts." If the phrase has any valid meaning, it applies to capitalism, because greater wealth is created under a division of labor, that is, through the production and trade of individuals interacting with each other, than through the self-subsistent production of isolated individuals on a desert island.

Individualism is a philosophic doctrine, beginning in metaphysics, that holds the individual entity as the primary unit of reality. What our minds initially perceive and know are individual concretes, from which each of us, as individuals, abstract universal characteristics and relationships to build our knowledge. On the basis of the universal knowledge we each have acquired, we then apply that knowledge to the individual, specific situations of our own lives, choosing values to pursue and trading value for value with others through mutual, voluntary agreement. Individualism leads to ethical egoism and capitalism. It starts from the fields of philosophical psychology, epistemology and psycho-epistemology, and theoretical and applied psychology, all disciplines that study the nature and functions of the individual mind.[33]

---

capitalism. There are not many others. An early work by Breggin is *The Psychology of Freedom: Liberty and Love as a Way of Life* (Buffalo: Prometheus Books, 1980).

[32] Probably because of the power of compartmentalization to prevent the proverbial right hand from seeing the implications of the left, political pun not intended, though it does apply.

[33] Philosophical psychology studies human nature (the core of which is the individual mind) and the place of humans in the universe; epistemology studies the nature, origin, means and extent of human knowledge; psycho-epistemology the interactions between the conscious and subconscious mind, especially their automatized processes; and theoretical and applied psychology are what today are usually labeled "experimental" and "clinical."

Epistemological Foundations

The problem with psychology today, as Branden stated pointedly in *The Psychology of Self Esteem*, is that the field "is in desperate need of epistemological rehabilitation." The claims of many of the theories, he says, are arbitrary and ponderously irrelevant. "The cause, both of the irrelevance and of the arbitrariness, is the evident belief of their exponents that one can have a science of human nature while consistently ignoring man's most significant and distinctive attributes."[34] And those distinctive attributes, as presented above, are the capacity to reason and the volitional nature of that capacity. As we shall see, the failure of psychologists to acknowledge these attributes and to build a theory based on them is epistemological.

In the years since Branden made the above statements, most of them applying to psychoanalysis and behaviorism, the "third force," an assortment of practitioners identified by Maslow, has more or less congealed around individual growth and self-control to achieve happiness. These practitioners usually acknowledge that we possess a consciousness and sometimes even talk about free will or choice. What they all lack, and still lack today, is what Maslow pointed out in 1962, namely a comprehensive theory of human nature. What is needed to develop this comprehensive theory is not so much an epistemological rehabilitation, as Branden puts it, as a *habilitation*, a solid epistemological foundation, which psychology has not ever had.[35]

To be sure, Aristotle is sometimes identified as a founder of psychology, and Freud did leave us with a comprehensive theory. However, the "experimental-positivistic-behavioristic" theory, to use Maslow's description of behaviorism and its progeny, over the

---

[34] Branden, *Psychology of Self-Esteem*, 36.

[35] Rehabilitation presupposes the existence of assets that need to be restored to their former glory, like the renovation of a long-neglected mansion. See Samenow on the distinction as applied to criminals who, if they want to "go straight," tend not to possess many assets. Thus, habilitation, not rehabilitation is what criminals most need. Samenow, *Inside the Criminal Mind*, 275. Psychotherapists seeking to help responsible citizens look for their patients' assets from which to help them build a happier life. Most do have assets, so rehabilitation is a more appropriate term when working with the responsible.

past one hundred years has produced enormous amounts of data, but little, if any, reliable theory.[36]

The Aim and Fundamental Method of Science

All theoretical sciences—whether physical, biological, or human—study the nature of entities, their attributes, and their actions. The entities may be planets or molecules, chimpanzees or amoebas, or human beings and the processes of their minds. The aim of science is to identify what is universal in the nature of the entities or attributes under study and the actions and interactions of those entities and attributes with other entities and their attributes. Thus, the primary aim of theoretical science is to *explain* by identifying universals.

Most, perhaps all, sciences have their applied or practical components and some entire sciences are considered applied or practical, deriving their basic principles from the more fundamental sciences on which they rest. Physics and biology are examples of fundamental sciences, while engineering and medicine are examples of applied or practical sciences. Thus, a second aim of science is to *guide*, to identify principles of action, to guide humans to choose the correct, practical means of achieving specific ends.[37]

The fundamental method of all sciences is said to be observation, but if we understand that conceptualization is a form of observation,

---

[36] And I am not claiming here to present a comprehensive theory. I am suggesting that psychology needs another Freud. Or rather, if Freud can be compared to Plato in philosophy, psychology needs a modern Aristotle to stand on Freud's shoulders. See Maslow, *Psychology of Being*, 7–8, for the "experimental-positivistic-behavioristic" designation. Maslow also uses the term "scientism," which in its significant usage means a "pretense at science," thoroughly examined in F. A. Hayek, *The Counter-Revolution of Science: Studies on the Abuse of Reason*, 2nd ed. (Indianapolis: Liberty*Press*, 1979), 24–25 and throughout. First edition published in 1952.

[37] Logical positivism assumes that values are subjective, so the two functions of science, according to positivism, are to explain and predict, not to guide action. Explanation, however, implies prediction and values are not subjective. Thus, the two aims of theoretical and applied science are to explain and guide, while the historical sciences use theory to *describe* past events, whether natural or human. See Ludwig von Mises, *Theory and History: An Interpretation of Social and Economic Evolution* (New Rochelle, NY: Arlington House, 1969).

because it presupposes the use of our senses, then conceptualization is the fundamental method.[38] For it is conceptualization of observed data that forms and defines universal concepts and identifies universal principles.[39] Systematic bodies of concepts and principles constitute our sciences; specific bodies of concepts and principles, unique to our own experiences, constitute our personal knowledge. The reality that human psychology studies—the objective reality—is that attribute of the entity, human beings, known as consciousness and the actions of that attribute.[40]

Conceptualization is universalization. Conceptualization is inductive generalization and does not require statistical samples to validate knowledge. Statistical projection, the primary method of positivism, is unsound and wasteful as a method of validating theoretical knowledge. When my daughter, for example, was not yet one year old, she saw a ball bounce and roll and laughed heartily. She did not need to observe a sample of five hundred round, spongy things bounce and roll in order to generalize that round, spongy things bounce and roll.

Similarly, neurologist V. S. Ramachandran, proponent of the value of individual cases in science, has remarked:

> Imagine I were to present a pig to a skeptical scientist, insisting it could speak English, then waved my hand, and the pig spoke English.

---

[38] This statement assumes that the senses are valid and that the analytic-synthetic dichotomy is not. See David Kelley, *The Evidence of the Senses: A Realist Theory of Perception* (Baton Rouge, LA: Louisiana State University Press, 1986); Rand, *Objectivist Epistemology*, 279–82; Leonard Peikoff, *Objectivism: The Philosophy of Ayn Rand* (New York: Penguin Books, 1991), 39–48; and Leonard Peikoff, "The Analytic-Synthetic Dichotomy," in Rand, *Objectivist Epistemology*, 88–121.

[39] And the two fundamental methods of observation, or conceptualization, are extrospection and introspection. Another way to classify the sciences is fundamental and derivative. The three fundamental sciences are said to be physics, biology, and psychology. Engineering derives its most basic principles from physics and the other physical sciences, medicine from the biological sciences, and all the human sciences, including economics and the applied business disciplines, from psychology. The most fundamental of all sciences is philosophy.

[40] There is far too much unnecessary equivocation over the use of the word "subjective" in psychology. Consciousness indeed is "in our heads" and therefore is subjective when compared to everything else that is outside of us, but as the object of study of psychology, consciousness is psychology's *objective reality*.

Would it really make sense for the skeptic to argue, "But that is just one pig, Ramachandran. Show me another, and I might believe you!"[41]

The skeptical scientist, typical of nearly all scientists today, insists that the only way to establish knowledge is to observe five hundred cases, or a thousand, or two thousand. Anything less is an isolated instance, often denigrated as anecdotal evidence or an individual case.

This skeptical approach to science has come about over the last two hundred years because David Hume failed to find a necessary connection between cause and effect and Immanuel Kant failed to find "true reality." Then, the logical positivists picked up the banner of science as the search for "successive approximations," not universals, followed by Karl Popper's criterion of falsifiability to dictate what constitutes genuine theory in contrast to mere pseudoscience. In the absence of a sound theory of universals statistical probability is said to be the only valid method of science.[42]

---

[41] Quoted in Norman Doidge, *The Brain That Changes Itself: Stories of Personal Triumph from the Frontiers of Brain Science* (New York: Viking Penguin, 2007), 178. I am not advocating "one-case generalization" with these two examples. My point is that not many instances are necessary to conceptualize perceptual concretes and their basic causal attributes.

[42] Karl Popper, *Conjectures and Refutations* (New York: Routledge & Kegan Paul, 1963), chap. 1. The chapter is based on a lecture given in 1953. Popper prefers "corroboration" to probability, but the latter has become the lingua franca of science. When put into terms of an objective theory of truth, Popper's falsifiability criterion means supported theories, hypotheses, and concepts must be shown capable of being contradicted, that is, shown capable of *incorrectly* identifying reality. Aside from the fact that Popper and his followers are claiming to know something about Kant's unknowable true reality (though Popper is careful not to endorse Kant's premise that the mind *imposes* laws on reality), and aside from all the concrete-bound, rationalistic and decidedly unscientific black swan and black raven puzzles to demonstrate the metaphysical certainty (not probability) of the criterion, falsifiability is at best irrelevant to science and at worst destructive of its true nature. It is irrelevant because the aim of science is to establish truth by demonstrating *correct identifications* of reality. It is destructive because it expects us to spend our time and resources generating "highly informative guesses" and then trying to prove them false before starting to look for truths. "The sciences, and scientists," says historian Peter Gay, "do not work quite like that. Solid positive evidence, whether gathered through responsible observation or in controlled experiments, remains the most eligible support that scientific claims can master." Peter Gay, *Freud for Historians* (New York: Oxford University Press, 1985), 64–65.

It is this premise that allows modern psychologists to dismiss the entire Freudian corpus, including the concept of repression, as unscientific, or worse, as pseudoscientific. Why? Because Freud's evidence is "anecdotal" and the "experimental-positivistic-behavioristic" methods of the physical sciences cannot validate his ideas. It is this premise that allows nearly all scientists to dismiss the notions of consciousness, free will, and introspection.[43]

Conceptualization Is Universalization. There is, however, a sound theory of universals: Ayn Rand's theory of concepts.[44] Rand's contribution to the theory of universals is her recognition that the essence of a concept is not "in the thing," as Aristotle assumed, nor is it arbitrary. The essential distinguishing characteristic of a thing is identified by omitting its measurements, or to use familiar words of psychologists, the "individual differences" of the many instances. Round, bouncy things can have different diameters plus various circumferences and volumes, all within a certain range of measurement, and can be made of a variety of materials, but they are still round and bouncy. That is the essence of a ball. The essence is universal and applies to all balls past, present, and future. Individual balls are identified by their varying measurements and materials, as well as their specific location in space.

The universal is now objective because we, using our rational, volitional consciousness, formulate and define it. At the same time, reality determines whether our formulation is correct or not. Logic, again, in the monitoring of our (internal) psychological premises, is our guide to the correct perception, identification, and integration of the (external)

---

[43] As with materialism and determinism, self-contradiction is rampant in logical positivism and its consequent dismissals of these three concepts. The positivists are using consciousness, free will, and introspection in their claims of denial. At root, positivism is just another theory of skepticism, which also is self-contradictory. Lest they collapse into an infinite regress, positivists must claim as a certainty that certainty is impossible.

[44] Rand, *Objectivist Epistemology*. Summaries of Rand's theory are available in Peikoff, "Concept-Formation," chap. 3, in *Objectivism*; Jerry Kirkpatrick, *In Defense of Advertising: Arguments from Reason, Ethical Egoism, and Laissez-Faire Capitalism* (1994; paperback ed., Claremont, CA: TLJ Books, 2007), 147–52; and Kirkpatrick, *Montessori, Dewey, and Capitalism*, 82–86.

facts of reality. Conceptualization as a process of universalization is based on Aristotle's formal cause, which says that an entity's actions are determined by its identity. Identifying universal relationships between entities and their actions give us principles and laws.[45]

Thus, my daughter's laughter at witnessing the round spongy thing bounce and roll was her conceptualization of the entity, by observing its essential distinguishing characteristic. Of course, she did not have words to describe the process at the time, but her mind, nonetheless, was processing her perception. The same can be said about Ramachandran's English-speaking pig (assuming no tricks of ventriloquism). One does not need a sample of five hundred English-speaking pigs to conclude that something quite unusual has just happened.

In Defense of "Anecdotal" Evidence and Individual Cases. "Anecdotal" evidence and the use of individual cases often are attempts to identify universals. They may be true or false or somewhere in between. Logic must guide. Conceptualization was the method of Aristotle—and Freud. Measurement is not the essence of theoretical science, though the data it provides can be necessary and helpful, to be sure, in the physical sciences, especially the applied, technological sciences. It also can be necessary and helpful in the human sciences, but free will precludes exact measurements of any kind.[46] Measurement in the human sciences provides only historical, not theoretical (universal), data.[47] Many, perhaps most, descriptive and so-called causal studies

---

[45] The post-Renaissance conception of billiard-ball causality (Aristotle's efficient cause) contributed in no small way to the so-called problem of induction and, especially, the lack of scientific confidence in the biological and human sciences.

[46] The doctrines of materialism and determinism, after all, do not correctly identify the facts of reality. Note that the algebraic equations of the physical sciences are universals that have omitted the measurements of the variables. Precise measurement in the physical sciences does give us more information, and this Aristotle and the Greeks lacked, but what the precision gives us is knowledge of the individual case. Measurement of the individual case is essential for technology or applied science. It enables us, for example, to send a spaceship to the moon, and then duplicate it later, perhaps with improved adaptations. It is not the essential distinguishing characteristic of theoretical science.

[47] Windelband's distinction between nomothetic and idiographic sciences has been debated in psychology for many years, but Windelband was right. Psychology is a nomothetic science that seeks to identify universal laws. Ludwig von Mises

in the human sciences, those that for decades have been mimicking the methods of the physical sciences, at best produce historical data, much of it trivial, some of it shallow, misleading, and false.

For example, studies of repression are contrived and fail to reflect the reality they are claiming to measure. One such study asked subjects to list pleasant and unpleasant experiences, then at a later time to recall what was on the list and write them down. More unpleasant than pleasant ones were left out of the reconstructions, so this allegedly demonstrated the presence of repression. However, critics pointed out that a stronger affect, which in this study meant the pleasant experiences, was more easily remembered. This meant that intensity of affect determined what was recalled or forgotten, not whether the experiences were pleasant or unpleasant. The presence of repression in this study, therefore, it was concluded, was not supported.[48]

This is not how conceptualization works. It is the requirements of statistics and controlled experimentation—the requirements of a certain sample size, the manipulation of a hypothesized causal variable (or effect), and a mechanism of measurement to enable statistical projection—that causes this superficiality. The definition of repression in these studies as "selective forgetting" is farcical, but that is what happens when concepts must be shoehorned into a rigid (and arbitrary)

---

clarified the distinction by separating the sciences into the theoretical and the historical. History, says Mises, looks at the individual case and identifies causes of individual events, which is exactly what psychotherapists do (and medical doctors and, of course, historians). Conceptualization remains the method used by both historians and therapists. I do not, however, agree with Mises that psychology should be separated into the experimental and the literary (or thymology). The correct distinction at root is Ayn Rand's: the metaphysical versus the man-made. Wilhelm Windelband, "Rectorial Address, Strasbourg, 1894," *History and Theory* 19 (Feb. 1980), 169–85. Mises, *Theory and History*. Rand, "The Metaphysical Versus the Man-Made," in *Philosophy: Who Needs It*, 28–41.

[48] Another study concluded that subjects with high anxiety and low social desirability, as measured by standardized self-report scales, were repressors. Critics, however, pointed out that denial, not repression, could have been operating. David S. Holmes, "The Evidence for Repression: An Examination of Sixty Years of Research," in Jerome L. Singer, ed., *Repression and Dissociation: Implications for Personality Theory, Psychopathology, and Health* (Chicago: University of Chicago Press, 1990), 85–102.

methodology.[49] Research in the human (and biological) sciences cannot and should not be modeled on the controlled experimentation of physics and chemistry.[50]

The best person to gather data on repression is a psychotherapist and the method of gathering the data, ironically, is "self-report," the same measuring technique used by most conventional psychologists. To be sure, the technique is not a standardized questionnaire, but an intelligence with the ability to conceptualize and make judgments about the accuracy of a patient's statements. It is this technique that the "men of hard science" dismiss as "clinical speculation."

Conceptualization is the fundamental scientific method because it generates identifications that are universal. The essential distinguishing characteristic of a concept identifies the universal nature of the instances subsumed under the concept. It was through his discussions with Josef Breuer about Anna O that Freud began to conceptualize, or rather, hypothesize, the presence of something operating in Anna O's mind that prevented her from remembering what might have caused or contributed to her illness. It took Freud time, and additional data from different patients, before he settled on the generalization called

---

[49] As I wrote in *In Defense of Advertising*, "Much of what passes today for theoretical research in the human sciences . . ., to the extent that it is valid at all, merely verifies the obvious and belabors the trivial,"163n50. Cf. Hurlburt on the seemingly endless cycle of "theory validation" in current psychological research that almost from its beginning is cut off from observational experience. Hurlburt is a lone and tireless researcher aiming at the rehabilitation of introspection in psychology, though, unfortunately, he continues to use the "experimental-positivistic-behavioristic" methodology. Russell T. Hurlburt, *Investigating Pristine Inner Experience: Moments of Truth* (New York: Cambridge University Press, 2011), 422–36.

[50] Branden's definition of repression: "a subconscious mental process that forbids certain ideas, memories, identifications, and evaluations to enter conscious awareness. Repression is an *automatized avoidance reaction*, whereby a man's focal awareness is involuntarily pulled away from any 'forbidden' material emerging from less conscious levels of his mind or from his subconscious" (Branden's italics). Branden, *Psychology of Self-Esteem*, 77. Repression is an automatized, standing order to avoid, whereas the creative process is an automatized, standing order to attend to and integrate anything relevant to the problem under study. Repression is the diametric opposite of creative thinking. Branden, *Psychology of Self-Esteem*, 80. See my discussion of repression below, pp. 144–47.

"repression." Freud did not originate the concept, but his formulation was decidedly significant, scientific, and empirical—about as empirical a scientific formulation as one can find in psychology today.[51]

By nearly exact parallel, to give one more example of scientific conceptualization, this time from biology, Jane Goodall was solo researcher sitting in the Gombe Stream Chimpanzee Reserve in Tanzania, observing the behavior of her "patients," the chimpanzees. She was, of course, dismissed by the "men of hard science" for, aside from being a woman and an uncredentialed one at that, so anthropomorphically and "unobjectively" assigning names to the chimps, and collecting nothing but anecdotal data. Goodall's "anecdotal data" included discoveries that chimpanzees eat meat, can configure and use tools to find food, and have personalities. This scientific knowledge was all acquired via conceptualization. Large samples and statistical projections, contrary to what the present-day positivists assert, are not required to establish knowledge.[52]

Measurement and Statistics Are an Aid to Science, Not Its Essence. Statistical projection—and the correct word is "projection," not generalization—has its place in our search for knowledge, but it does not replace scientific induction. Statistical inference, as it is also correctly called, projects a finding from a sample to a population. Thus, if data in a sample of 500 American men show that two percent have red hair, and the research did not commit any flagrant methodological

---

[51] Freud also had to differentiate repression from defense mechanism, which, according to his daughter, Anna, he did not finalize until 1926. Anna Freud, *The Ego and the Mechanisms of Defence*, trans. Cecil Baines (New York: International Universities Press, 1946), 45–46. First published in German in 1936. See Freud on his discussion that anxiety is a feeling that the mechanism of repression attempts to combat. Sigmund Freud, *Inhibitions, Symptoms and Anxiety*, trans. Alix Strachey (New York: W. W. Norton, 1959), 34–40. First published in German in 1926.

[52] Jane Goodall, *In the Shadow of Man* (1971; New York: Mariner Books, 2000). Henry Nicholls, "When I Met Jane Goodall, She Hugged Me Like a Chimp," *The Guardian*, April 3, 2014, https://www.theguardian.com/science/animal-magic/2014/apr/03/jane-goodall-80-chimp. In biology, the higher non-human animals, because they possess a consciousness similar to that of humans, clearly have some modicum of choice and ability to learn and problem solve. Presumably, though, they do not have the ability to regulate their mental processes, which is what we call free will, or self-awareness.

errors, then a projection (or inference) can be made, within a margin of error, that two percent of men in the entire country have red hair.

A projection moves from *some to some*—from two percent of the sample to the same two percent in the population. A scientific generalization, on the other hand, when, for example, forming a concept of round, spongy things that bounce and roll, or of human beings who possess the capacity to reason, moves from *all to all*.[53]

All of the balls I have observed bounce and roll; all humans that I have observed possess the capacity to reason. Therefore, all spongy balls, past, present, and future, by their very nature, bounce and roll. The same conclusion is drawn that all humans possess the capacity to reason. Statistical projection assists scientific research. It is not a substitute for it.[54]

Freud's method was conceptualization. His aim was to define universals.[55] We do not have to accept everything Freud said, and he did say many wrong things, to acknowledge his accomplishments. His primary achievement was a presentation of the first comprehensive theory of psychology. We do not have to accept his theory of the unconscious and its drives, or the id, the ego, and the superego, or his focus on the

---

[53] I am using "induction" and "generalization" as synonyms. The modifier "scientific" is redundant.

[54] The place of statistical projection, as I have written before, is only in contexts in which we do not know, or cannot know, universal laws to explain observed data. The former means we are working with insufficient knowledge to formulate a law, the latter means we are working in the human sciences in an area where free will is operating. Free will precludes the possibility of identifying mathematically precise laws of human behavior. Kirkpatrick, *In Defense of Advertising*, 156–58. The primary use of statistics in experimentation is control, that is, the statistical control of sources of extraneous variation.

[55] See John P. McCaskey, "Induction in the Socratic Tradition," in *Shifting the Paradigm: Alternative Perspectives on Induction*, ed. Louis F. Groarke & Paolo C. Biondi (Berlin: De Gruyter, 2014), 161–192, on his efforts to revive Socratic induction, a tradition promoted and debated both before and after Francis Bacon, but eventually overtaken by the nineteenth-century positivistic, Millian hypothetico-deductive method, a form of rationalistic, propositional inference of going from particular statements to universal statements. Socratic induction—generalization from particular things or concretes to universal abstract ideas—is consistent with Ayn Rand's epistemology as inductive concept formation through measurement omission.

libido or Oedipal complex, and we certainly do not have to accept his materialism or determinism—to appreciate his greatness.[56] Freud was looking for universals, and he found a few, not just repression, but also defense mechanisms, to use his words, and the significance of subconscious influence on present behavior. According to Szasz, Freud's greatest contribution to psychotherapy "lies in having laid the foundation for a therapy that seeks to enlarge the patient's choices and hence his freedom and responsibility. . . . Although never clearly articulated, the aim of psychoanalytic treatment was, from the start, to 'liberate' the patient."[57]

THE EGOISM OF PSYCHOLOGY

This brings us back to the individualism of psychology. Freud's aim was to liberate the patient from painful inhibitions and painful symptoms, manifested most often as what he called defense mechanisms. The removal of these inhibitions and symptoms would enable the patient to become more autonomous, self-responsible, and independent. Freud laid the groundwork for the later psychotherapies that now help individual patients seek a happier life. Although also not articulated by Freud, but central to his theory, Szasz continues:

---

[56] See Bruno Bettelheim, *Freud and Man's Soul* (New York: Vintage Books, 1984), especially 4–8, 53–64, 71–78, 89–94, for his case to retranslate Freud in less "abstract, depersonalized, highly theoretical, erudite, and mechanized" and often Latinized language that pretends to make him more "scientific." Such new translations, says Bettelheim, would present Freud as he is in the original German, more human and eloquent. Examples of mistranslations, according to Bettelheim: *drive* should be used instead of instinct; the *it*, the *I*, and *above-* or *over-I* (as retained in French and Spanish translations) instead of id, ego, and superego; *parry* or *fend off* instead of defense; *repulse* or *rebuff* instead of repress; *faulty achievement* or just *slip* instead of parapraxis; *energy* or *charge of energy* instead of cathexis; and, especially, *soul* instead of mind. Freud, says Bettelheim, viewed psychology as the science of the soul and frequently used the German word for soul, not mind. "Soul," says Bettelheim, for Freud is "that which is most valuable in man while he is still alive." Bettelheim, *Freud and Man's Soul*, 77. Nathaniel Branden defines soul as "a man's consciousness and his basic motivating values." Branden, *Psychology of Self-Esteem*, 132.

[57] Thomas Szasz, *The Ethics of Psychoanalysis: The Theory and Method of Autonomous Psychotherapy*, (Syracuse, NY: Syracuse University Press, 1965), 16.

Psychoanalysis is meaningless without an articulated ethic. . . . It is a model of the human encounter regulated by the ethics of individualism and personal autonomy. The aim of psychoanalytic treatment is thus comparable to the aim of liberal political reform. The purpose of a democratic constitution is to give a people constrained by an oppressive government greater freedom in their economic, political, and religious conduct. The purpose of psychoanalysis is to give patients constrained by their habitual patterns of action greater freedom in their personal conduct.[58]

Psychology, by its very nature, is individualistic—and egoistic. And, as stated at the beginning of this chapter, one would expect that the contemporary advocates of humanistic psychology, those therapists who put an emphasis on free will, individual self-realization, and personal growth and fulfillment, guided by the goal of lessening or removing obstacles to happiness, would be advocates of individualism and capitalism.

An indication of what prevents psychologists today from connecting their field to capitalism can be seen in statements of Maslow. In addressing implications of the term "self-actualization," Maslow lists what he considers to be several shortcomings. Selfishness is number one. Shirking duty and neglecting ties to other people and society follow close behind. These shortcomings puzzle Maslow because the self-actualizers he studied seemed to him to be "altruistic, dedicated, self-transcending, [and] social"[59]

Maslow's puzzlement, however, as well as his colleagues' lack of perceived connection to individualism and capitalism, stems from centuries of cultural thinking dominated by religion and, in the last century-and-a-half, by Marxism and other forms of secular altruism. Yet in philosophy, egoism is not identical to the Hobbesian sacrifice of others to oneself. It only means, as it did to Aristotle and Spinoza, concern for one's welfare. And that would include breathing and eating, two decidedly selfish actions without which we would all die.

Maslow is correct. Self-actualization is indeed selfish, in the good, not Hobbesian, sense. So is the exercise of one's free will. So is the desire

---

[58] Szasz, *Ethics of Psychoanalysis*, 17–18.
[59] Maslow, *Psychology of Being*, 5.

for personal growth and fulfillment. So is the goal of lessening and removing obstacles to one's happiness. Shirking duty? Self-actualizers are shirking duty only if that word is taken to mean self-sacrifice. Self-actualization is the opposite of sacrifice. Self-actualizers are responsible citizens, which means they make commitments and do not fail to meet them. Self-actualizers do work hard, often alone, but they are not anti-social. This is the religious and leftist mythology that follows ethical egoism wherever it is espoused.

Even William Glasser's "reality therapy" and "choice theory" are highly individualistic and self-interested approaches to helping people with psychological problems and, more generally, are prescriptions for conflict-free social relations. The former seeks to help patients solve reality- or fact-based problems in the present to achieve happiness.[60] The latter is Glasser's broader theory of how people relate to one another, namely that optimal relationships result from reality-based choices to control only one's own behavior, not that of others, which last cannot be peaceably accomplished. Focusing on one's own internally controlled choices and behavior, says Glasser, brings people closer together, while attempting to practice external control moves them further apart.[61] It is difficult to see how Glasser's approach does not fit the classically liberal society of Ludwig von Mises. Yet Glasser insists that his work has always been politically and religiously neutral; he was not an advocate of laissez-faire.

Despite Glasser's insistence, we find this statement of independent judgment in his 1976 book *Positive Addiction*:

> As we grow, we should learn to judge for ourselves what is worthwhile, but it takes a great deal of strength to do what is right when few people will agree with us for doing it. Most of us spend our lives in a series of compromises between doing what we believe in and doing what will please those who are important to us. Happiness depends a great deal on gaining enough strength to live with a minimum of these compromises.[62]

---

[60] William Glasser, *Reality Therapy: A New Approach to Psychiatry* (1965; repr. New York: Harper & Row Perennial Library, 1990), 6.

[61] Glasser, *Choice Theory*, 4–26, 57–61.

[62] William Glasser, *Positive Addiction* (1976; repr. New York: Harper Perennial, 1985), 3.

Making our own fact-based judgments and acting on those judgments, regardless of what others, significant or not, may say about our choices and behavior, is the essence of independence. Exclusively internally controlled choices and behavior are egoistic and individualistic. They are required for individual happiness and for peaceful relationships with others. They are the basis of a free society.

It is to the fundamental psychological requirements of a free society that we now turn. There does seem to be a significant connection between the theory and practice of psychology and capitalism.

3

The Psychology of Independence

Independence is the recognition of the fact that yours is the responsibility of judgment and nothing can help you escape it—that no substitute can do your thinking, as no pinch-hitter can live your life.

—John Galt[1]

The essential psychological requirement of a free society is the willingness on the part of the individual to accept responsibility for his life. . . . [It is] a strong sense of personal identity [that] leads to the individual becoming self-responsible, and that in turn increases the likelihood that he will want to live in a free society.

—Edith Packer[2]

PSYCHOLOGICAL HEALTH AND HAPPINESS depend on learning and exercising independent judgment. The development of independent judgment depends on freedom—in the home, in the school, and in society.

Healthy, happy citizens feel sufficiently worthy, self-reliant, and competent to perceive the world as it really is and to exhibit the integrity and courage to act on those perceptions in speech and action. In whatever walk of life they happen to work or play, healthy, happy citizens are unafraid to see and say that the emperor has no clothes.

---

[1]Rand, *Atlas Shrugged*, 1019. Galt, again, is the hero of Rand's novel.
[2]Edith Packer, "The Psychological Requirements of a Free Society," in *Lectures on Psychology*, 249–50.

Sometimes an independent judgment may go against the will of the majority or the convictions of family, friends, or colleagues, but toleration of such convictions is precisely what defines the free society and powers it to new heights of freedom and accomplishment. Giving in, succumbing to fear, wearing blinders, going along with the status quo, and other forms of compromising what we see, and are willing to say and do, thwarts happiness by undermining our sense of identity and compels us to resort to compensating behaviors. Self-confident, happy contrarians and dissidents are the ones who fuel the innovation and intellectual and material progress on which a free society thrives.

Not everyone, though, has to be a contrarian or dissident. Unlike the statistical impossibility of everyone being above average in ability or intelligence, everyone can exhibit and express the independent judgment of the boy in the Hans Christian Andersen tale. Curiosity for subtle detail is precondition, as is refusal to deviate from the perceived facts. Speaking the truth and standing behind the truth through action is consequence.

PERSONAL IDENTITY AND SELF-RESPONSIBILITY

According to Edith Packer, "The essential psychological requirement of a free society is the willingness on the part of the individual to accept responsibility for his life."

> This means that [each individual] alone has to make all the decisions concerning his life. He must choose and identify his values; he must make such decisions as what career he will choose, where he will live, what goods he will purchase, and so on—his life is not planned for him at all. . . . If most people in a society are unwilling or afraid to accept this responsibility, a capitalist society cannot come into being—or, if somehow it did come into being, it will not last. People will simply not want it.[3]

That is, each individual must develop a strong personal identity and practice independence. As a psychologist, Packer then asks, "how does [each individual] come to value and enjoy self-responsibility?"[4]

---

[3] Packer, "Psychological Requirements," 249–50.
[4] Packer, "Psychological Requirements," 250.

Note that self-responsibility is not a chore or a duty or a self-sacrifice. It is a value and a virtue. Psychologically, it is, or should be, a conflict-free pleasure. It is to the development of a psychology of independence that we now turn.

The Aloneness of Independence

A strong personal identity is built up slowly from childhood, decision by decision, choosing values that make one feel "this is who I am," not who my parents, relatives, or friends want me to be. Self-responsibility is the implementation of a personal identity by making commitments to provide for oneself, both existentially and psychologically, then fulfilling those commitments. Existential responsibility is what we normally think of as independence in the adult world of moving away from home and working at a job to pay our bills. Psychological responsibility, however, is more challenging. It means making commitments to understand our psychology, thereby more fully developing self-esteem to maintain and enhance our mental health and happiness.

Psychological responsibility requires the aloneness of independence. "Aloneness," as used here, does not mean lonely. It means no one can get inside anyone else's head to make that person think or not think, to make such a person evade by putting his or her head in the sand or face reality, whatever that reality may present, promising or threatening. This also is the meaning of a self-created personality. Neither genes nor environment (which last includes our parents as a significant part of our genetic makeup and early environment) have created who we are psychologically. They have influenced us, but we are our own self-programmers, as Ayn Rand puts it; we mentally process everything we are exposed to.[5] This means something is going on in our minds every waking minute of the day—that is, not just thoughts and the processing of knowledge, but evaluations, emotions and their corresponding action tendencies, memories, and fantasies and daydreams. And our nighttime dreams, as Freud said, are products of our current or past

---

[5]Rand, "Objectivist Ethics," in *Virtue of Selfishness*, 23–24.

daytime mental activity. Each of us alone (in contrast to what Freud said) creates the contents of our own consciousness.[6]

The orderliness of human consciousness varies from person to person, depending on how well each has programmed the mental content. The orderliness also depends on how much control each person has in the present over how he or she processes newly confronted events. This brings us to the issue of subconscious influence on present perception.

The Components of Our Psychology

Each of us alone creates the contents of our own subconscious, with one exception.

Our brains are organs of integrating action, "connection-making machines," as I put it guardedly in an earlier work, meaning that new, not-directly-controlled-by-us subconscious content can result from these connections.[7] When awake and asleep, connections are being made—sometimes bizarre ones when asleep, sometimes new and insightful ones when working on a creative project, which can occur when either asleep or awake. Other connections can contribute to psychological health and happiness, deriving, for example, from the habit of strictly adhering to facts, or to inhibitions to health and happiness, deriving from defense values and other defensive habits.

The brain's integrating action is physiological, but it works with the material and standing orders we give it. When awake, we control

---

[6] Freud's unconscious id consists of drives or impulses that are present at birth and influence us throughout our lives. The id, says Freud, is a "dark, inaccessible part of our personality." It is "a chaos, a cauldron full of seething excitations" and "untamed passions." Sigmund Freud, *New Introductory Lectures on Psycho-Analysis*, trans. and ed. James Strachey (New York: W. W. Norton, 1965), 91, 95. First published in German in 1933. The aim of therapy, according to Freud, is to tame the chaos. Freud's concept of an inborn id that affects us in the present classifies him primarily as a genetic or biological determinist. Environment, of course, through the superego and external world also play an influential role. The notion of an irrational inner self driving and controlling us goes back at least to Plato's allegory of the chariot, though even that predates Plato. *Phaedrus*, 245c-257b.

[7] Kirkpatrick, *Montessori, Dewey, and Capitalism*, 86. I emphasize that "connection-making machine" is a metaphor "with no concessions to mechanistic materialism intended."

its actions through reason and logic.[8] Thus the integrations we make when awake can be logical or illogical, depending on how well from an early age we have noticed, assessed, and organized the material available to observation and depending on how logical or illogical the standing orders are that we have issued.

Whatever we are currently aware of is conscious, though our current awareness may be divided, say, into a highly focused and intense conversation while driving the car, on the one hand, and the highly automatized skill of driving, on the other. Awareness of how to drive the car is present in our conscious mind, but our awareness of the skill is low; we are functioning, as it were, on "autopilot," driving by habit and according to standing orders, such as "drive defensively."

Whatever we are not currently aware of on any level is subconscious, including the name of a movie that could not be recalled during the "focused and intense" conversation and the skill of driving when we are not driving or thinking about driving. Everything in our subconscious is potentially conscious and retrievable, or can be inferred, when the right skill is applied.[9] The subconscious is the storehouse of

---

[8] It seems we can control the content of our dreams by giving ourselves commands at bedtime, say, not to dream about a specific event or thought, or to practice what today is called lucid dreaming. Von Domarus, drawing on Freud's concept of primary process as description of the illogic of dreams, schizophrenics, and young children, hypothesized that at least in part the subconscious makes connections according to the fallacy of the undistributed middle. This prompted Arieti to call the functioning of the subconscious paleo-, as opposed to Aristotelian, logic, the latter being what gives us control, properly used, of our conscious minds. E. von Domarus, "The Specific Laws of Thought in Schizophrenia," in J. S. Kasanin, ed., *Language and Thought in Schizophrenia* (Berkeley: University of California Press, 1944), 104–14. Silvano Arieti, *Interpretation of Schizophrenia*, 2nd ed. (New York: Basic Books, 1974), 229. First edition published in 1955.

[9] Truly forgotten material, most likely from the first two or three years of our lives, is apparently not available to be retrieved. In the absence of brain damage, memory still fades over time but, again, depending on how well our minds are organized, the emotional impact of a given event, and the extent to which we are committed to reason as our means of knowledge, we may be able to recall events, premises, and knowledge with accuracy or we may blur or even fabricate them. On the malleability of memory, see Julia Shaw, *The Memory Illusion: Remembering, Forgetting and the Science of False Memory* (London: Random House Books, 2016). Memory researchers, unfortunately, in their efforts to deny the existence of repressed memory also tend to deny the existence of repression itself as a defensive habit.

all our integrated, automatized knowledge and experiences.[10] From the standpoint of psychology, certain key judgments and experiences define who we are and the extent of our mental health and happiness. These key judgments and processed experiences constitute the components of our psychology.

Core Evaluations, Elaborated. Core evaluations, as summarized in the previous chapter, are fundamental subconscious conclusions (evaluations) formed in childhood about ourselves, other people, and the world in general (reality).[11] They are held as self-evident truths and operate as automatized habits to influence our future development and present actions. Self-esteem is formed as a cluster of core evaluations, based on our mental choices and physical actions over time, plus other less fundamental, mid-level evaluations. Specifically, self-esteem is our conviction of worthiness and efficacy. Sense of life is the emotional sum and expression of our core evaluations and self-esteem.

The following discussion presupposes a definition of mental health that is neither physiological nor deterministic. Edith Packer states that mental health is "the ability to deal with a set of facts in any given context

---

[10] By analogy only, and continuing with Rand's notion of humans as self-programmers, our subconscious is the central processing unit of a computer that works only as well as we have programmed it. Habits, good and bad, are its output. It is not Freud's unconscious, nor is it, strictly speaking, our memory, though the two are related; nor is it certain connections our brains make that produce products we can consciously become aware of or infer, but never create ourselves, such as percepts automatically generated from sensations or specific emotions automatically generated from specific evaluations. These automatic connections are physiological and out of our control; they should not be considered sub- (or un-) conscious. Other connections, we can and do control through consciously determined current or standing orders. What is subconscious is what our conscious minds at one time produced or allowed to be produced with or without conscious instructions. See Linda Reardan, "Emotions as Pleasure/Pain Responses to Evaluative Judgments: A Modern, Aristotelian View" (Ph.D. diss., Claremont Graduate University, 1999), 30–31. Cf. John R. Searle, *Mind: A Brief Introduction* (New York: Oxford University Press, 2004), chap. 9. If our conscious instruction is inaccurate and our subconscious is disorganized, we may mistakenly think Freud's id is controlling us. Branden's definition of the subconscious: "the sum of mental contents and processes that are outside of or below awareness." Branden, *Psychology of Self-Esteem*, 66. I submit that "outside of" should be removed from Branden's definition, leaving only "below" as the appropriate modifier.

[11] See above, pp. 67–69.

in the present without preconceived or hidden automated subconscious motivations." Neurosis, in contrast, "is the inappropriate expectation of injury in the present," where "inappropriate" means "there is no basis in reality for such expectation."[12] Mental health requires correct, that is, rational, core evaluations, but also correct, rational mid-level and concrete evaluations, all of which contribute to the development of a correct, rational self-esteem. The resulting sense of life and personality will then be one of confidence and independence. Failure to make correct, rational evaluations—which usually occurs only in certain areas of our lives, more areas for some people, fewer for others—leads to the many familiar psychological symptoms and defensive maneuvers that indicate problems in living, such as the seemingly objectless fear called anxiety, as well as depression, withdrawal, hostility, denial, rationalization, displacement, acting out, and so on.

Core evaluations are "few in number—probably less than ten," says Packer, formed early in life usually by emotional generalization, not conscious choice. Core evaluations are then held subconsciously to influence our futures. And all of us are capable of holding, and often do hold, contradictory core evaluations, correct and rational ones along with those that are mistaken. "Mistaken core evaluations," continues Packer, "are at the root of all defense mechanisms and most out-of-context emotions. They are at the base of all neurosis." Core evaluations are the "autopilots" of our lives, habits and standing orders for good or ill, that guide the way we process new experiences, make choices, and act.[13]

---

[12]Packer, "Understanding the Subconscious," 2 (Packer's italics omitted). Cf. Branden, *Psychology of Self-Esteem*, 99: "Mental health is the unobstructed capacity for reality-bound cognitive functioning—and the exercise of this capacity. Mental illness is the sustained impairment of this capacity" (Branden's italics omitted). Note that both Packer's and Branden's definitions of mental health are biological in the Aristotelian sense, not physiological as in the medical model. Branden described his psychology as "biocentric." If we understand the meaning of "biological in the Aristotelian sense," we should consequently not feel uncomfortable calling ourselves a "patient" when visiting the psychotherapist. We are, after all, seeking help in achieving mental health ("human flourishing" or *eudaimonia*, to use Aristotle's word). The substitute "client" in today's parlance does not capture the nature of the relationship.

[13]Packer, "Understanding the Subconscious," 4–5.

Emotional generalization, to further elaborate the process, begins with reactions to specific events, say, a father yelling at and calling his son a klutz (or worse) for spilling a glass of milk. The child may feel fear and anxiety for having done something wrong and probably hurt at the way his father reacted to the objectively harmless event. Similar events repeated over time, may lead the child (the child's subconscious integrating actions) to generalize the fear and hurt to other people, such as teachers, and in adulthood, to all other people he comes in contact with. The integrating actions, unexamined by the young child, see similarities between father, teachers, and others who yell. A core evaluation becomes established in the subconscious and automatized as, perhaps, "I can't do anything right. I must be careful around other people."

It is important to emphasize and to clarify that this is not environmental determinism. The child could have reacted differently to the spilled milk and name-calling father. And some children do react differently in such situations, by saying to themselves, for example, "What's the big deal? I didn't do it on purpose. Father is being ridiculous!" Better teaching—of the parents, teachers, and other adults who yell at children and call them names when they make mistakes—would go a long way in countering the development of this and other similarly negative core evaluations. The adult needs to help the child process the event, not make the situation and the child's psychology worse.[14] Haim Ginott's advice, paraphrased, is appropriate here: "Oh, the milk spilled. Here's a sponge. Let's clean it up and get you another glass."[15]

The ease with which children can draw mistaken conclusions indicates how important it is for their parents and other adults to be there for them, to support them, by finding out what is going on in their minds. In particular, they need to help children put words to their emotions by identifying the thoughts and evaluations that stand behind the

---

[14] Packer, "Understanding the Subconscious," 10–11. See in Packer, 11–12, and below in the present work, chap. 5, pp. 141–43, for a mistaken core evaluation that was caught in the making by the child's mother.

[15] Ginott, *Between Parent & Child*, 51–52. What Ginott is recommending is that we describe the problem and offer constructive help without evaluating the child.

feelings. This requires trust and intimacy. Unfortunately, says Packer, "most children do not share many of their important thoughts and emotions with their parents," or other adults. Core evaluations, both good and bad, build up brick by brick as "hundreds and hundreds" of concrete experiences.[16]

Using a different analogy, Packer describes core evaluations as "the trunk of a tree," with the branches representing mid-level evaluations that are narrower and formed later in our development, such as judgments about our ability to participate in sports, our competence at academic schoolwork, our choice of career interests, and our sexual self-confidence in relation to ourselves as a male or female and to the opposite sex. Core and mid-level evaluations then influence and reinforce one another.[17]

For example, two broad, sweeping core evaluations, such as "I can't do anything" and "I'm no good," will produce serious consequences in later development about one's competence in sports and schoolwork. Core evaluations, on the other hand, that say "I can do most anything if I put my mind to it" and "I am a worthy person" will likely produce opposite, more correct and rational mid-level judgments and will establish a path in adulthood toward a mentally strong and healthy personal identity, along with a sense of self-responsibility.

Just as core and mid-level evaluations influence and reinforce one another, core evaluations in the three fundamental areas of our lives—self, others, and the world—interact by influencing, reinforcing, and generalizing evaluations from one area to the other two. For example, a child who concludes "I can only expect injury from other people" may go on to conclude that "something is wrong me" and "the world has little to offer me."

The significance of core evaluations is that our subconscious applies them in the present to every new concrete experience remotely similar to the ones that gave rise to the core evaluation in the first place, "without our permission in the present," to quote Packer's choice words.[18]

---

[16]Packer, "Understanding the Subconscious," 12, 10.
[17]Packer, "Understanding the Subconscious," 5, 14.
[18]Packer, "Understanding the Subconscious," 7.

The "leaves" of Packer's tree analogy are quite specific evaluations, such as our tastes in food and clothing and where we would like to live. The "leaves" are nonetheless influenced by the "branches" and "trunk," and the "branches" and "trunk" are influenced by the "leaves." None is isolated from the other, but the concreteness of the "leaves" means they are more easily changed, and often are. However, the "leaves" are still tied to the "branches" and "trunk," for example, the concrete evaluations that "I'm not smart enough to go to this college," "I'll probably choose the wrong dish from tonight's menu," and "my outfit is ugly." Core and mid-level evaluations are most likely operating in these three concretes.

Mid-level and core evaluations become firmly embedded in our subconscious, especially by adulthood. While many of us can usually be aware of our specific evaluations and, to some extent, our mid-level ones, most of us are not aware of core evaluations. The "hundreds and hundreds" of concrete experiences that evoked emotions in us as a child are largely forgotten. The painful emotions, and sometimes even pleasant ones, are repressed. As an adult, many of us have no clue why we feel what we feel and act the way we act. This lack of introspective awareness is what makes us vulnerable to the genes-environment arguments.

Mistaken core evaluations, because of their clash with reality, cause out-of-context and painful emotions. Eventually, if not corrected, they lead to defense values and other defensive habits. A young man, for example, may be terrified at the prospect of asking a young woman for a date, even when friends point out that she will not bite his head off and perhaps also that she is all but throwing herself on him. Objective reality is clashing with this young man's core evaluations, and it is the core evaluations that prevent him from seeing the facts of what his friends are saying. Similar young men have even developed the defensive habit of withdrawal, thus ensuring that they will not put themselves in situations where they might meet members of the opposite sex, or in severe cases potential friends of the same sex.

Conflicts, such as the one described above, set up clashes like "I must but I can't" or "I want to but I can't" or "I want to but I mustn't."

These clashes mean something is not right. And the something is one or more mistaken core evaluations. Mistaken core evaluations, says Packer, must be made conscious and changed. Otherwise, they will continue to operate automatically and the conflicts will get worse. Prevention or correction of mistaken core evaluations at a younger age would have been the preferred solution to the subsequent conflict, but that would have required better teaching by adults at the child's younger age, which would likely lead to better subsequent choices by the child.[19]

Mental health is the ability to act in the present without hidden (subconscious) motivations that cause unfounded (non-objective) expectations of injury. The independent personality is a mentally healthy personality, whose core evaluations about self, others, and the world are, for the most part, correct and rational. As consequence, such a personality's mid-level and concrete evaluations will also, for the most part, be correct and rational. In the absence of omniscience and omnipotence, however, even the most healthy among us may reach adulthood with mistaken evaluations; such a personality will nevertheless know how to introspect sufficiently to monitor and correct mistaken evaluations of any kind. The independent personality knows and understands how to make the subconscious conscious.

Self-Esteem. The genus of self-esteem is confidence, the degree of certainty we have about something or someone. The something can be within us, such as a conclusion we hold about ourselves in general, or about an ability to perform a specific activity. We can possess high or low confidence in the truth of our knowledge and high or low confidence in the skills we perform. We can also have high or low confidence in another person to perform certain actions.

Self-esteem pertains to ourselves, our psychologies, so it is the degree of confidence or certainty we have in ourselves as a valuable person and as someone competent to correctly and rationally choose values and actions to make us happy in life. The two interacting and

---

[19] Packer, "Understanding the Subconscious," 8–10. Cf. Branden, *Psychology of Self-Esteem*, 72–77, 160–65, and Allan Blumenthal, *Identity, Inner Life and Psychological Change* (self-pub., CreateSpace, 2013), 67–74.

reinforcing components of self-esteem are worthiness and efficacy. Both are mental, that is, psychological, not existential or physical as in our high or low competence in changing a tire, though existential competencies derive from and are influenced by the mental ones.

A primitive form of worthiness and efficacy can be seen operating in the newborn infant who, if put on his or her mother's stomach, will succeed in crawling up to the breast. Such a feat requires the implicit conviction that "My life is valuable, so I must seek and find my source of food." Self-esteem consists of the convictions, "I am worthy" and "I can do it." This inborn primitive self-esteem can be encouraged and developed or hampered and damaged by parents and other influences of the child's environment.

The worthiness component of self-esteem is our certainty that we are valuable to ourselves, that we are our own highest value. Self-worth and self-respect are synonyms. This makes worthiness fundamentally egoistic; demands for self-sacrifice undercut it. If we value ourselves highly, we can easily value ourselves in addition as capable of being valued, that is, loved, by others. The source of this self-worth initially comes from the infant's mother, then also from the father and other significant adults in the child's surroundings. Holding and touching, plus verbal expressions of love, interact with the infant's self-esteem to provide the warmth and security that young, as well as older, children need.[20]

This means that around age two—the "terrible twos"—when children begin to assert themselves (sometimes opposing adults, sometimes just asserting their developing self-confidence), verbal abuse, such as yelling, name-calling, and irrational commands like "don't be selfish," plus physical abuse, including spanking by hand, are often experienced by the child as humiliating, or even threatening. These traditional techniques of child-rearing are the primary early influences that lead children to develop negative core evaluations, especially self-doubt

---

[20]Essentially, this is an attachment theory, but absent the genetic or environmental determinism. Cf. John Bowlby, *Maternal Care and Mental Health* (Geneva: World Health Organization, 1951).

about themselves, but also fear of others, and confusion or even negative conclusions about the world in which they live. Today's permissive
directionless parenting is just as bad, if not worse, because of the psychological chaos it creates.

It is here that Maria Montessori's advice to "control the environment, not the child" is especially perceptive, the only exceptions to her
maxim being intervention to prevent children from harming themselves
or others. Montessori's advice is meant to continue into the schools
and throughout the child's upbringing. Unconditional love from significant adults encourages the development of self-worth. The result
is the certainty of being a good, moral person deserving of happiness.

The efficacy component of self-esteem is cognitive competence,
the certainty that we can and do perform the actions necessary to use
our minds properly, to identify rational values and act to acquire them.
"Actions necessary to use our minds properly" means an unconditional
commitment to reason and facts. This commitment requires us to
monitor the contents and functioning of our conscious and subconscious minds. It means introspection to identify the nature, meaning,
and cause of our emotions, which ultimately means to identify and
correct any mistaken core and mid-level evaluations. Introspection
must continue throughout our lives.

The two components of self-esteem influence and reinforce each
other, so a high self-worth encourages and supports strong competency, and vice versa. Alternatively, low self-worth undercuts one's
competencies, and vice versa. High self-esteem is an accomplishment
that has to be earned over many years and sustained with persistent
monitoring. It is not experienced as a brag or boast, for example, as
Packer puts it, "Boy, I'm a great, worthy [and competent] person." That
is not self-esteem. "Rather, self-esteem is experienced as a total emotional state" that gives us "a certain calm and a sense of control—as if
the most important issues about [ourselves are] settled." Self-esteem
is a quiet confidence. Its emotional expression is pride.[21]

---

[21] Packer, "The Art of Introspection," in *Lectures on Psychology*, 230.

98 • Independent Judgment and Introspection

If put into words, a healthy self-esteem would say something to the effect, "I am confident that I am valuable to myself and others, deserving to be loved—by myself and others—as the honest and independent person I am. I am also competent to use my mind in a correct, rational way to make me happy in life."[22] In Packer's words, self-esteem says, "I am basically fit for life. I do not have to doubt that fact." Doubting oneself, or self-doubt, is expressed as the emotion of anxiety. Anxiety then is what generates our need for defensive maneuvers to defend against the unpleasant feeling.[23]

But as Packer is fond of saying, self-esteem, along with many other psychological phenomena, is a continuum. Self-esteem is not an either-or skill in the sense that either we have it or we do not have it. We can have high self-esteem, which means high confidence, or medium self-esteem with some self-doubt and anxiety, or low self-esteem and a lot of self-doubt and anxiety. And most of us probably have high self-esteem in at least one area of our psychologies, but medium and low self-esteem in other areas. Our challenge to achieving mental health and happiness is to be aware of the contents of our conscious and subconscious minds in all areas and correct the errors in thinking that we might find.

Sense of Life. Core evaluations and self-esteem determine who we are as individuals. Sense of life expresses our identity as an emotional sum, a composite set of emotions that outwardly expresses our outlook on life. As Ayn Rand says, it is a "pre-conceptual equivalent of metaphysics." Metaphysics studies the fundamental nature of reality and our place in it, so the "pre-conceptual" part of our sense of life is our core evaluations from childhood formed through emotional generalizations that express who we are and what we think about other

---

[22]Mruk calls this "the two-factor theory" of self-esteem and attributes it to Nathaniel Branden. Christopher J. Mruk, *Self-Esteem Research, Theory, and Practice,* 3rd ed. (New York: Springer Publishing, 2006), 19. First edition published in 1995. Mruk points out that the concept of self-esteem in psychology goes back to William James and that both Sigmund Freud and Alfred Adler were aware of its significance. Mruk, *Self-Esteem Research,* 12–14.

[23]Packer, "Art of Introspection," 230.

people and the world in which we live. Sense of life, according to Rand, "becomes a generalized feeling about existence, an implicit *metaphysics* with the compelling motivational power of a constant, basic emotion—an emotion which is part of all [our] other emotions and underlies all [our] experiences."[24]

Sense of life is what an artist projects in a work of art and what patrons of the arts respond to. If it could be put into words, a sense of life would say, from the artist's perspective, "this is life as I see it," and from the patron's viewpoint, "this is how I do or do not see life." Sense of life attracts and repels, so sense of life is what one falls in love with, or does not fall in love with. Sometimes, in experiencing an instant like or dislike of someone we meet, it is our sense of life meshing or clashing with the other person's sense of life.

According to Packer our sense of life gives off "emotional vibrations," so an astute observer of emotions might say, to use her examples, "that person is eaten up with envy" or "that person really loves life and is at ease with himself." The recipients of these verbal observations may react with the impression that the "astute observer" has just read minds, though that is not the case. What is happening is that sense of life broadcasts strong clues about the nature of our core evaluations. What the observer may pick up in the other person is an impressionistic sense that "life is an adventure" or that "happiness is not possible."[25]

Sense of life, however, it must be emphasized, is a composite emotion and emotions are not infallible. Getting to know another person, whether as a friend or romantic partner, requires time and patience to explore and learn all of the other person's values, ranging from the philosophical and abstract to the everyday and concrete. Judging another person is even more difficult. Judging whether another person is honest and independent requires close interaction before a reliable conclusion can be drawn. Sense of life only gives clues, both to one's own subconscious and to that of others.

---

[24] Ayn Rand, "Philosophy and Sense of Life," in *The Romantic Manifesto: A Philosophy of Literature* (New York: Signet Books, 1975), 25–26 (Rand's italics).

[25] Packer, "Understanding the Subconscious," 9, 4.

THE INDEPENDENT PERSONALITY[26]

Personalities are distinctive, characteristic ways of thinking and acting. The independent personality is one that is guided exclusively by facts, not obstructed by internal inhibitions or easily deterred by external, environmental constraints. The dependent personality experiences self-doubt and unreasonable (objectless) anxiety in many areas of life, but especially at the prospect of having to stand alone and disagree with or challenge the opinions and desires of other people. As a result, such a person is ruled in varying degrees by those opinions and desires. The independent person, of course, does consult the opinions and desires of others and enjoys relationships, personal and business, but does not experience an irrational anxiety in the process of disagreeing with or challenging those others.

Independent personalities exhibit a strong personal identity and commitment to self-responsibility. This means they hold positive core and mid-level evaluations and have high self-esteem, that is, a high confidence in their worth as a person and in their ability to guide their lives exclusively by reason, which includes monitoring their mental processes for errors and correcting the errors. The astute observer of emotions may even pick up the quiet confidence or "life is an adventure" sense of life of an independent personality. The independent personality of high self-esteem, to repeat an essential point, does not brag or boast.

How do we come to value and enjoy self-responsibility? A strong personal identity is prerequisite, and this comes from positive core evaluations. "The key to personal identity," says Packer, "is values. The more developed, integrated, and intensely held are a person's values, the stronger is his sense of identity." No one is born with a personal

---

[26]The following discussion is based on Edith Packer's identification of core evaluations as fundamental to our development and will be at best an outline of the independent personality. What is needed in the field of psychology is a treatise on independent judgment derived from a career's worth of psychotherapeutic observations made by a therapist (or therapists) who have focused on the psychological development of independent personalities. Biographies do not satisfy this requirement, as they usually do not spend much time on their subject's childhood or exhibit psychological sophistication. Until such a research project is undertaken and the subsequent treatise is published, the present outline must do.

identity. It is self-created, starting with our core evaluations in the three fundamental areas of our lives.

About ourselves, we must hold the conviction that we are worthy of happiness, that we have control over our lives, and that we accept our uniqueness as an individual. This means we have adopted an "internal control" psychology, to use Glasser's words. We do not blame external events and obstacles for our failures, or complain about other people who seem to get in our way. We constantly strive through our own self-motivation to find ways around the obstacles. Accepting our uniqueness means we accept who we are, that is, we are not at war with any attribute of ourselves, such as height, looks, gender, or intelligence. While some attributes can be changed or improved, and it is important to know what can be changed realistically and what cannot, acceptance of what is changeable and what is not is necessary for confidence. Ruminating about or denigrating our looks or intelligence is not conducive to high self-esteem.

About other people, our conviction is benevolent and holds that they are a source of pleasure. Although there do exist a small percentage of people who are criminals, manipulators, and bullies, most are kind, decent, and capable of a sincere rationality. This means we give others the benefit of the doubt until we see evidence otherwise. We do not sacrifice ourselves to others, nor do we expect others to sacrifice themselves to us. In a division of labor society, force and fraud are out; cooperation by trading value for value is what defines equality in relationships. The medium of exchange can be money, our labor, products, or simply the pleasure of another's company and conversation, based on mutually shared values. No one is dominant or subservient, or manipulative or manipulated. Glasser's deadly habits that destroy relationships are out.[27]

About reality, our conviction is that the world in which we live is comprehensible, that in principle our minds are capable of

---

[27] Glasser's deadly habits that destroy relationships, to repeat from chapter 1 of this work, are "criticizing, blaming, complaining, nagging, threatening, punishing, and bribing (rewarding to control)." Glasser, *Unhappy Teenagers*, 13

understanding any aspect of the universe. Nothing is unknowable. Though we certainly are not omniscient and do not know many things, and we are dependent on the state of science and technology to aid us in our quest for knowledge, we can, if we put our minds to it, learn and understand whatever it is within our reach and skill that we are putting our minds to. The world is not a mysteriously haunted house or orderless chaos, but a place of adventure. As Packer says, the world "is not something to be feared and avoided, but rather something to be explored, understood, and conquered."[28]

The most significant value that expresses one's identity and firmly implants a sense of self-responsibility is productive work. Productive work is the creation of value primarily for oneself, but also for exchange with others in the marketplace. Level of ability and intelligence is not relevant, as the value created can range from the knowledge and skill of driving a truck to the creation and management of a billion-dollar enterprise. What is relevant is that the choice of work be out of love, not a chore, duty, or defensive attempt to please significant others. From the standpoint of psychology, a realistic self-assessment of our abilities, intelligence, and preparation for chosen career is essential for taking responsibility of our lives. For someone who has never played tennis before, for example, a desire at age twenty or thirty to become a competitor on the professional circuit is not likely to be fulfilled, and probably results from deeper psychological issues, such as mistaken core and mid-level evaluations. A change of career in one's forties, however, which may include more years of education, can and often does occur.

Other values express and reinforce the confidence that our lives are self-created and that we are self-responsible. Abstract, philosophical values, such as honesty, integrity, courage, and above all a commitment to reason, logic, and facts must be absolute. But more specific, concrete values in the areas of leisure, friendship, and romance round out the expression of our identity. The sense of "this is me" runs throughout everything we do. If it does not run throughout and we start to feel "this

---

[28] Packer, "Psychological Requirements," 252.

is not me" or "something is not right," we probably should reexamine our values and consider changing one or more of them. *Enjoying* self-responsibility, as opposed to sacrificing ourselves for the sake of duty, or simply to please others, is what is required for a confident, independent, and happy life.

Three additional values, says Packer, are essential for translating our values into reality. One is a commitment to initiative and achievement, to take action to accomplish our goals, as opposed to excessively daydreaming about what we would like to do someday. A second value is perseverance and hard work; this may include a requirement to learn a new skill or an advanced degree, as opposed to succumbing to self-doubt and giving up. The third value is tolerance of failure, which means not interpreting a failure as a personal inadequacy.[29]

The significance for a free society of a strong personal identity and sense of self-responsibility is that these traits form the essence of psychological independence, which in turn promotes an eagerness to pursue one's values without external control—which means without interference from others who might violate our rights. This in particular means the government. The notion of a free society—laissez-faire capitalism—presents opportunities to the independent personality, opportunities to demonstrate competence and ability and be rewarded for the effort.

A dependent personality, one who has not developed a strong personal identity, sense of self-responsibility, and consequent confidence in one's worth and competence, reacts with fear to the prospect of capitalism—because capitalism offers no guarantees and expects all physically healthy citizens to care for themselves. Capitalism is a psychological threat to dependent personalities because they do not feel they can take care of themselves. They feel helpless and think they need someone else to provide for them.[30] If citizens of a society are not

---

[29] Packer, "Psychological Requirements," 258–61.

[30] A few who feel extremely helpless will choose to control others and become manipulators and criminals. Some criminal personalities may choose to work in government and become tyrannical bureaucrats or, in the extreme case, dictator of the country. In other cases of extreme helplessness and insecurity, withdrawal from family and society can lead to breaks with reality, otherwise known as

willing to assume responsibility for themselves, a free society cannot come into existence. If it does, it cannot last.

Let us now look at the dependent personality.

THE DEPENDENT PERSONALITY

Dependent personalities are the ones who go along with the other adults in the story of "The Emperor's New Clothes" and cheer the Emperor's decidedly missing wardrobe. They may even actively attempt to silence the boy who points out the truth of the Emperor's nakedness. Although under certain circumstances there can be objective threats to an independent personality to justify "going along in order to get along," such threats, at least in a free society, are often more psychological than existential.[31]

The "facts" of reality that dependent personalities spend much of their time observing are other people, usually a specific group of significant others, though it can be anyone. The dependent personality's identity derives, to the extent that such a person is dependent, from what those others believe, value, and do. Self-doubt and internal inhibitions, such as defense values and other defensive habits, motivate them. Their mental focus is almost always toward other people. Judgments of fact and value are obtained from the others and are therefore made "second-hand," not independently by using their own minds alone focused on the reality of the problem. "Second-hand," dependent judgment results from fear of what thinking for ourselves and identifying and asserting the truth might mean.[32]

---

psychotic episodes. For those who truly suffer mental and physical deficiencies that prevent them from caring for themselves, the free society does not inhibit or block charity from families and eleemosynary organizations. Historically, in pre-Progressive nineteenth century United States, there was no shortage of such help.

[31] For example, if the Emperor says he will execute all adults who make negative comments about his new clothes, that would indeed be an objective threat. This is the Socrates issue, "Do we have to die for our independence?" to be discussed in chapter 4. (In the Andersen story, the Emperor is convinced by the con-artist weavers that those who cannot see his new clothes are unfit for their positions in the court or are just stupid.)

[32] Ayn Rand identified the notion of "second hander" while working in Hollywood in the 1930s. She observed the behavior of an ambitious woman who always

Dependent personalities, to use sweeping generalizations, can be described by stating the opposite of what represents the independent personality.[33] Dependent personalities aim to minimize anxiety, so they choose undemanding work or less demanding work than they are capable of. They may view work as drudgery, living for the weekend. They may choose friends and associates they can feel superior to and who share their negative view of the world. They do not tolerate failure and often settle for less than they deserve or actually desire. Severely dependent people are often envious of what others have, because they feel incapable of achieving what the people they envy have achieved or of acquiring what the others have acquired.[34]

Dependent personalities gravitate to groups as the source of their identity, such as their religion, nation, race, class, ethnicity, or private clubs.[35] They gravitate to the government as their caretaker.[36] Even moderately independent people who do not support capitalism claim they want welfare for the poor, but not for themselves. Says Packer, they reveal their dependence when they admit they want the government to be there for themselves "just in case" they need to be taken care of. Dependent personalities, concludes Packer, are prime candidates for

---

compared herself to other people, wanting and valuing what those others wanted, only more so, not what she in a first-hand manner wanted. "Second hander" became a significant concept in Rand's novel *The Fountainhead*. Barbara Branden, "A Biographical Essay: Who Is Ayn Rand?" in Nathaniel Branden, *Who Is Ayn Rand* (New York: Random House, 1962), 192–93. "Social metaphysics" is the psychological term coined by Nathaniel Branden. Metaphysics studies the nature of reality, "first hand" through independent thinking. "Social metaphysics" is a method of perceiving reality through the filter of what other people think and value. Social, not objective, reality, is the psycho-epistemological focus of dependent personalities. Branden, *Psychology of Self-Esteem*, 171–77.

[33] Packer, "The Role of Philosophy in Psychotherapy," in *Lectures on Psychology*, 205–208.

[34] Packer, "Psychological Requirements," 261–65.

[35] On the premise that "likes attract likes," dependent personalities are more comfortable with other dependent personalities, and a group is more comfortable than the "aloneness of independence." (Criminals, who are dependent personalities in a worse way than the ones I am describing, befriend other criminals, though, as I stated earlier in chapter 2, they trust no one.)

[36] Packer, "Role of Philosophy," 206.

socialism because they fear self-responsibility. "Such people want to be taken care of, and in return they will gladly obey. A nation that breeds a dictator is a nation of people who are afraid of life."[37]

The "ultimate validation of capitalism"? Capitalism's "psychological requirements," says Packer, "are also the requirements of life and happiness." That means a strong sense of personal identity and commitment to self-responsibility. "[Capitalism] is the only system consistent with the requirements of human life."[38]

Prisoners of Childhood

The source of our adult psychologies is our childhood experiences, the conclusions we drew in response to the many events we confronted. To the extent that we drew correct, rational conclusions in childhood, to that extent we put ourselves on the path to an independent personality. To the extent we did not draw those correct, rational conclusions, to that extent we put ourselves on the path to dependence and unhappiness. Accordingly, dependent personalities can be described as "prisoners of childhood," to borrow the phrase from Alice Miller. Or as Packer puts it, they are pursuers of infantile needs that were not satisfied in their earlier years.[39]

The most significant needs relevant to the formation of an independent or a dependent personality are safety and security. Parents and other adults who fail to satisfy these infantile needs may vary widely in their behavior, from coldness or unemotional distance to meanness

---

[37] Packer, "Psychological Requirements," 264. Cf. Greenberg, *Crisis in American Education,* 54: "Dependence, not independence, is the quality most suitable to authoritarian states. . . . The hallmark of the independent man is the ability to bear responsibility. To be responsible and accountable for one's actions. To do, and to stand up for what one has done. Not to hide behind 'superior orders,' not to seek shelter in group decisions, and to take strength from some heroic figure—but to be one's own man." The aim of Greenberg's Sudbury Valley School in Massachusetts is to instill independence in his students. Greenberg, however, is not an advocate of laissez-faire capitalism and the independence encouraged is existential, not psychological.

[38] Packer, "Psychological Requirements," 265.

[39] Packer, "Psychological Requirements," 261–65. Miller, *Drama of the Gifted Child.* Miller, though, apparently is an advocate of environmental determinism.

and physical abuse, but the child's conclusions and subsequent core evaluations in reaction to such influences probably will say something to the effect, "I am helpless," or "No one will protect me." To the child, feelings of helplessness and consequent low self-esteem are experienced as life-threatening.

Most, perhaps all, children in such situations will resort to defensive maneuvers to assuage the fear, self-doubt, and anxiety. The goal of the maneuvers is to find, or attempt to find, protection and satisfaction of the infantile needs they did not get in childhood. Thus, the defensive habit of repression attempts to prevent children from feeling pain and helplessness. When this does not work, denial may be adopted. Or compulsive work habits in school and later in adult life may be pursued to demonstrate to their parents (even after the parents may have died) that they are worthy of their parents' love. Many other coping actions may follow.

The process, of course, does not happen all at once, but builds up over the years as children mature toward adulthood. The aim of maturation is individuation and independence from parents. Failure to find satisfaction of safety and security needs, however, leads to the development and solidification of a dependent personality as an adult.

As Packer states, "A dependent person may select God, the State, or Significant Others as the source of his protection. Even a mild form of dependence can find expression in all areas of a person's life—in his work, his political ideas, his dealings with people, and his selection of values in general."[40] And choice of romantic partner, Packer continues, is also often the dependent person's attempt to find protection. When one or both partners is dependent on the other, unhappiness will be the result.[41]

To repeat, these independent-dependent personality descriptions are not either-or. Most of us did not grow up in perfect familial or other caregiving environments, nor did we make all the right choices. Most

---

[40] Packer, "Role of Philosophy," 206.
[41] Packer, "Role of Philosophy," 206–207.

of us will exhibit independence in some areas of our lives and dependence in others, and this will vary from person to person. For example, it is not uncommon to meet someone who is accomplished in his or her profession but unhappy in personal life. The pursuit of infantile needs in the area of romance will often explain the unhappiness. All, or nearly all of us, as a result, grow up with a split mental focus, partly on reality, because that is the world in which we must live, and partly on other people. To the extent that we pursue our unsatisfied infantile needs, to that extent we will be dependent on those others to give us what we did not get in childhood.[42]

Relying, however, on God, state, and significant others, including our romantic partner, for what we did not get in childhood does not work. Uncorrected core and mid-level evaluations will spread and our split focus will undercut our health and happiness. Defensive maneuvers are like drug highs that can temporarily blunt our pain, but the pain will return. Much of the operation of defense values and other defensive habits works subconsciously to erode our sense of worth and competence in the reality-focused areas of our lives. To the extent that we are dependent, therefore, we will experience difficulty appreciating or desiring a free society.

The solution for our dependent, or any other unhappy, personality is introspection to identify and correct our subconscious core and mid-level evaluations, then action on the basis of the new, corrected rational evaluations.

The Anti-Conceptual Mentality

In *Montessori, Dewey, and Capitalism* I discussed Ayn Rand's "anti-conceptual mentality" as a type of mental passivity that needs to be challenged by educators. In its place students need to be encouraged to develop a mentally active mind, that is, a "pro-conceptual mentality."

---

[42]The split focus can have more than one cause, such as the defensive habit of compartmentalization and a lack of knowledge and skill, say, in conducting relationships. On the psychology of, and skills required for, lasting romantic relationships, see Packer, *Lectures on Psychology*, chap. 5 and 6.

The concept as Rand uses it, I stated, is too moralistic, and today I would say too intellectualized in the sense that it places too much emphasis on conscious control over subconscious influence, but it does indicate an important trait of the dependent personality.[43]

Rand defined the anti-conceptual mentality as a mind that is passive "in regard to the process of conceptualization and, therefore, in regard to fundamental principles. It is a mentality which decided, at a certain point of development, that it knows enough and does not care to look further."[44] The "which decided" part is what is too moralistic. Even though there is a choice involved in all of the conclusions we draw in childhood, many early ones are formed as emotional generalizations and later ones are strongly influenced by our already formed subconscious, which means the choices are difficult for us to be aware of and prevent or change at the moment they occur. This is the meaning of subconscious influence on our present choices and behavior, and Ayn Rand acknowledged that she did not understand psychology. This is why I say that her concept places too much emphasis on the conscious over the subconscious. The notion is valid in essence, but it also does not express enough psychological understanding.

The anti-conceptual, dependent personality is one that stops at a certain point of development and goes no further. The stopping point, or most likely, the point at which learning slows down markedly, is a "comfort zone" against anxiety that is provided by the group of significant others. As psychologies vary widely along a continuum, the stopping point and group can be one's extended family or drinking buddies . . . or colleagues of the same political, religious, or philosophical orientation. What happens is that this personality stops growing and fixates on whatever the group says and does, the goal of which is to fit in. Challenging the cherished beliefs and behavior of the group would cause discomfort. The coping habit of this group

---

[43] Kirkpatrick, *Montessori, Dewey, and Capitalism*, 184–87.
[44] Rand, "The Missing Link," 45.

association is often a defense value, the pseudo-self-esteem of setting oneself up as superior to outsiders and special in the eyes of the group's insiders. The psychology of this way of processing reality is group conformity.[45]

Independent personalities do not stop learning. They continue to form concepts and principles in all areas of their lives and do not hesitate to challenge orthodoxy of any group if the facts dictate. If the pull of group conformity is felt, independent personalities introspect to examine their premises and correct the mistaken ones.

DEVELOPING AND SUSTAINING INDEPENDENCE

Developing and sustaining psychological independence in today's cultural environment is not easy. How can we improve the culture? Independent parents who are happy together and schools that teach independence as their primary aim would be an ideal beginning.

Unfortunately for some children, many parents become separated and divorced, passing their lives through multiple unhappy relationships and by their role modeling encourage children to adopt negative core evaluations, such as "happiness is not possible" and "other people cannot be trusted." A commitment to happiness as a birthright and practice of the skills of happiness, along with trust of other people are prerequisites to teaching psychological independence to children.

Traditional parents who remain married during the children's formative years and use authoritarian methods of child-rearing, including the use of corporal punishment, can encourage the adoption of negative core evaluations. So can permissive or relativistic parents who use the "anything goes" approach to child-rearing that fails to teach values, manners, and sound principles of action. These parenting techniques are in need of reform with an emphasis on sound psychology.

---

[45] Branden, *Psychology of Self-Esteem*, 146. Religion and its conception of sin to induce guilt and shame, thereby encouraging mental passivity, plays no small role in the development of this group conformity. Cf. Carol Dweck, *Mindset: The New Psychology of Success* (New York: Ballantine Books, 2008), for a popular discussion of fixed versus growth mindsets, two traits, respectively, of dependent and independent personalities, though Dweck does not identify them as such.

Traditional schools teach obedience to authority, not independence. Permissive schools, in the absence of standards and guidance and in the presence of the chaos that results from their relativism, often by default teach obedience to authority. The imposition of authority in permissive situations is needed to restore order. Independence is a casualty, if we can even assume that independence is an aim in these schools, which in many it is not.

Maria Montessori's schools are a rare exception that holds independence as the aim of education. And it is not just existential independence that Montessori teaches. She makes an important contribution to the teaching of positive core evaluations, especially competence, but also indirectly worthiness. Each time a child completes a task of Montessori's didactic materials the child concludes, "I can do it." This is a developing sense of psychological efficacy. That the work in a Montessori school is performed without coercion, grades, exams, or degrees, that is, with an emphasis on freedom in the classroom, further encourages and reinforces each child's developing confidence in his or her worth.

I describe Montessori's process of "normalization" in *Montessori, Dewey, and Capitalism*:

> An important discovery of Montessori's is that certain psychological problems disappear when children are allowed to pursue their own interests in a prepared environment that stimulates concentrated attention. This is her concept of "normalization." Deviations or defects of character, as Montessori refers to these problems caused by interfering adults, such as rowdiness, possessiveness, and indolent passivity, vanish when the child becomes interested in a didactic material and begins to concentrate on it. After a short time, anxiety is replaced by inner calm and purposefulness. Outwardly, patience and a respect for others develops, because such a child learns to appreciate the absorption of others in these materials and is now willing to wait until a desired material is free. Confidence and self-esteem are the results of the normalizing process of concentrated attention.[46]

---

[46] Kirkpatrick, *Montessori, Dewey, and Capitalism*, 67. See also Montessori, *Absorbent Mind*, 201–07, 223, and Montessori, *The Secret of Childhood*, trans. M. Joseph Castelloe (1936; repr., New York: Ballantine Books, 1972), 154–76. First published in Italian in 1936.

Concentrated attention—absorption in a didactic material, or strong focus—is the aim of a Montessori education. It is Montessori's means to the end of independence. Freedom in the classroom is prerequisite, that is, freedom to move around the classroom and to choose which materials to work with.

Interestingly, current and former Montessori teachers say that they can readily spot a Montessori child (current or former)—by the concentration, effort and commitment to hard work, and initiative to proceed to the next task without having to ask or be told what to do. A strong personal identity and a sense of self-responsibility seem to be psychological results of a Montessori education. A culture of Montessori kids would go a long way toward establishing a culture of independence and thereby a shared desire for a free society.

Much more, however, to encourage this cultural environment needs to be done, especially in the area of psychological awareness, which means introspection to identify and correct one's philosophical and psychological premises, which in particular means the cause of our emotions and core and mid-level evaluations. This topic will be reserved for chapter 5. In the next we will address a number of mistaken conceptions of independence.

4

Mistaken Conceptions

> Thousands of years ago, the first man discovered how to make
> fire. He was probably burned at the stake he had taught his
> brothers to light. . . . Centuries later, the first man invented
> the wheel. He was probably torn on the rack he had taught his
> brothers to build.
>
> —Howard Roark[1]

> I want to emphasize now only the most important requirement
> of independence: the person's conscious and subconscious con-
> viction that he alone is responsible for his life.
>
> —Edith Packer[2]

MUST WE DIE FOR OUR INDEPENDENT JUDGMENT? Is it practical to be independent all the time? Doesn't life require compromise?

The first question is the Socrates issue. Socrates was a decidedly
independent thinker in ancient Athens and he ruffled many feathers
for his independence. So much so that he was condemned to death
by hemlock. He was offered a chance to escape and live in exile, but
refused. Should he have accepted the offer and would he be moral to
do so? This is a Philosophy 101 question asked of many students in
college classrooms.

---

[1] Ayn Rand, *The Fountainhead* (New York: Bobbs-Merrill, 1943; repr. Signet, 1971),
679. Roark is the hero of Rand's novel.
[2] Packer, "Role of Philosophy," 206.

114 • *Independent Judgment and Introspection*

The second and third questions above, in the first paragraph, raise more general issues, but they are still connected to Socrates. For example, if Socrates escapes, he is said to be compromising his principles and being less than independent. The only way to remain moral, according to this way of thinking, is to do one's duty and die.

Such an argument, of course, is absurd and derives from the deontological theory of ethics that says consequences must never be considered when determining ethical behavior. After all, the Bible says "do not lie," without making provisions for extenuating circumstances or consequences. Socrates followed his duty as an Athenian citizen, remaining "independent" to his death.

The secular altruists, guided by a secularized Immanuel Kant, say much the same thing as Socrates and the Christian altruists, but Kant has thrown us an additional curve, namely that the nature of our minds is such that consciousness distorts our perceptions of reality. As a result, there is no way we can discover whether or not we are judging and acting independently because we cannot and do not perceive facts. We can only guess what the facts are or infer them. Perhaps with the help of the "experimental-positivistic-behavioristic" scientists as our guides, we can accumulate mounds of data and through their epistemology of "successive approximations" gradually get closer and closer to reality. We'll never get there, though, because of the misrepresentations created by our minds.

Independence? Independent judgment? Independent action? Never happen. No one is an island, after all. At best we can accomplish the everyday sound judgment that is called wisdom. Political implications? Capitalism is out. Democracy is in—in the sense that we must talk things over and vote, and most importantly, rely on experts who seem to be able to know best what we should be doing.

Let us now consider several popular but mistaken conceptions of independence.

THE SOCRATES ISSUE

Democracy killed Socrates.

Socrates was convicted by vote in an Athenian court on the charges of impiety and corruption of the youth. He was then also condemned to death by vote.

The concept of rights was extremely limited at the time and applied only to Athenian citizens, which meant men, not women, children, slaves, or resident aliens. Socrates was a citizen, so he was entitled to a trial. Plato's dialogue *Crito* tells the story of Crito's offer to finance his friend's escape into exile. Socrates rejects the offer.

Socrates' argument is familiar still today. He said that it would be unjust for him to break the laws of Athens that he has agreed to obey. The citizen's relation to the state, he said, is the same as that of a child to a parent or slave to a master. This is an appeal to the omnipotence of the state and an implicit social contract that binds citizens to the laws of the land.

The answer to Socrates comes from the modern tradition of individual rights as defined by John Locke and clarified by Ayn Rand, especially Rand's principle that no one may *initiate* the use of physical force against anyone. This especially applies to government to whom one's right to self-defense in non-emergencies has been delegated for protection. So if a law is unjust, if it initiates force against citizens, retaliatory force in self-defense by citizens can be supported. For example, it is just for a citizen to break an unjust law—provided one is willing to accept the consequences, as in civil disobedience, or is willing to live in exile, as occurred during the Vietnam War era when young men moved to Canada to avoid the military draft's involuntary servitude. In extreme cases it is just to start a revolution of secession, as occurred in colonial America.[3]

---

[3] Civil disobedience does not mean breaking a law that has no connection to what you consider unjust, for example, blocking a street intersection to protest a minimum wage law or blocking entry to a venue to prevent patrons from hearing a speaker. Both are criminal acts. The former is a flagrant violation of property rights (even if the intersection is "owned" by the government) and the latter of both property rights and freedom of speech. Neither action is remotely close

Socrates should have gone into exile. The state is not omnipotent and the social contract is only a metaphor, a bad one at that.[4]

Thus, we do not have to die for our independence. Nor do we have to tell the truth when our privacy or other rights are being threatened. Living under a dictatorship with secret police forces and civilian informants is certainly a situation of initiated force. Surviving under such conditions where truth-telling could result in jail or execution requires ingenuity, such as speaking to trusted family and friends in a language that the spies and snooping neighbors are not likely to understand.

Even in a semi-free country such as the United States where education is dominated by government-initiated coercion, there is nothing wrong in encouraging students to "give teachers what they want," then telling the students to study on their own to develop ideas that may not be acceptable to the government-controlled schools. Free expression and free thought, contrary to pretensions otherwise, are not endorsed by the government-run "citadels of reason."[5]

As Ayn Rand said, "morality ends where a gun begins." So where the gun begins, we can lie our heads off and still be moral.[6] The issue is a practical one. If lying to a thief who demands the location of our money could lead to harm or death, because the thief does not believe us, it would be unwise—impractical but moral—to lie. The same applies to government initiators of coercion. Compromise of principles is

---

to civil disobedience, which means to accept the consequences of one's actions and perhaps also to test the issue in court.

[4] Social contract was an attempt to explain the origin of the state, but it is a fiction. More likely, powerful nomadic tribes conquered the weaker ones to establish control, and later conquered the settled farmers. The state holds the legal monopoly on the use of physical force. Its origin is in violence and coercion, not agreement. The aim of rights theory was and has always been to restrain and delimit government power. See Franz Oppenheimer, *The State: Its History and Development Viewed Sociologically* (New York: Bobbs-Merrill, 1914) on the state's origin and a first distinction between economic and political power.

[5] See Ludwig von Mises, *Bureaucracy* (New Haven: Yale University Press, 1944), 82–83, on how academic freedom in German universities meant freedom to agree with the government, which is essentially what it means in the United States today.

[6] Rand, *Atlas Shrugged*, 1023. The full statement, spoken by Rand's hero, John Galt, reads: "Force and mind are opposites; morality ends where a gun begins."

unethical, but when under duress, as the Anglo-American legal system allows, self-defense becomes the guiding principle.[7]

The challenge in living under duress, in a dictatorship or in the coercive environment of government-run schools, is psychological. The challenge is to maintain one's independence while putting on a front for protection. This means maintaining one's conviction to understand thoroughly the facts of any given situation—or in a student's case, the facts and truth of an assignment—while on the surface seemingly making concessions to the dictatorship or government school. Galileo recanted to the Inquisition, but did not sacrifice his scientific convictions. Faust, on the other hand, made a compact with the devil—and lost his soul.[8]

THE KANTIAN ISSUE

Kant killed reality and, as consequence, independence.

The Kantian issue, as Ayn Rand so aptly caricatured it, claims that we are "blind because we have eyes" and "deaf because we have ears."[9] Kant's argument is that our minds and senses have a specific nature such that by their very nature they prevent us from knowing reality. The identity and contents of consciousness, in other words, is such that it clouds and distorts whatever we have claimed to perceive. Reality may be out there, but we cannot know it. All that we can know are appearances or phenomena. That is the world we live in.

If we cannot know reality, we cannot know facts, which means we cannot be independent. But that's fine for Kant, because as an

---

[7]Making concessions in a business negotiation is not a compromise of principles, because both parties have accepted the principle of trade. Nor is it a compromise to accompany one's spouse to attend an opera, though you may not like opera. The mutually accepted principle is one of love and shared values. See Ayn Rand, "Doesn't Life Require Compromise?" in *Virtue of Selfishness*, 85–88.

[8]I thought of my years in graduate school as an exercise in "reinventing the wheel," in the sense of rejecting everything said in class and the texts, then slowly, after much thought and additional study, taking back what I judged to be true, and altering the false to correct formulations. I admired Galileo, not Faust. See Kirkpatrick, *Montessori, Dewey, and Capitalism*, 149–67, 190–92.

[9]Rand, *For the New Intellectual*, 32.

unwavering Protestant his philosophy was designed to save religion and religious ethics, that is, to "deny *knowledge* in order to make room for *faith*."[10] This process of "denying knowledge" made room for his severe ethics of self-sacrifice, namely to act solely according to duty, never from inclination. Altruism and self-sacrifice are retained as one's highest moral code and any form of egoistic independent judgment or action must go.[11]

The Kantian issue derives from the centuries-old failure of philosophy to understand the relation of existence to consciousness and to develop a sound theory of universals, among other problems. Kant complicated matters with his pre-Darwinian religious metaphysics that views humans as children of God, not naturalistic animals. The problem for us today is that post-Kantian and post-Darwinian philosophies have failed to develop an understanding of the relation of existence to consciousness or to present a theory of universals, nor have they taken seriously the relation of humans to animals, the relationship that could get them out of their rationalistically dug holes.[12]

Consider the higher animals—dogs, cats, chimpanzees—with whom we share certain attributes, the most distinctive of which is consciousness. Dogs, cats, and chimpanzees sniff and taste—and look at—reality. They do not live in a phenomenal world. Consciousness is the tool by which they perceive the world they live in and consciousness guides their choices and actions. They feel emotions, know a few words when

---

[10] Immanuel Kant, preface to second edition, trans. and ed. Paul Guyer and Allen W. Wood, *Critique of Pure Reason* (Cambridge, UK: Cambridge University Press, 1998), 117 (Kant's italics). First edition published in German in 1781.

[11] Kant's explicit aim was to save "*God, freedom* [free will] and *immortality*," as well as the religious, altruistic morality. To accomplish his aim he had to "*deprive* speculative reason of its pretensions to extravagant insights" (Kant's italics). Kant, *Critique of Pure Reason*, 117.

[12] Rationalism is a psycho-epistemology that focuses at length on deductive reasoning unconnected to reality, at the expense of the correct identification of facts, that is, truth. The doctrine of pure and perfect competition in economics is a prime example. See my discussion of the doctrine in Kirkpatrick, *In Defense of Advertising*, 118–26 and chap. 6. See also Kirkpatrick, *Montessori, Dewey, and Capitalism*, 74–76, 92–95, for my discussion of rationalism. Ayn Rand captured the absurdity of rationalism in economics when she said its implicit premise is: "Man is that which fits economic equations." Rand, "What Is Capitalism?" 7.

spoken to by humans, and can communicate with members of their species and with us through sounds and behavior. What they do not and cannot do is form universal concepts and write scientific treatises. Anthropomorphism, this is not.

The higher animals are simply functioning on a less advanced level than humans, but they are performing the same functions. Their consciousness is conscious of existence, which last is primary. They may not have an understanding of universals, but they do assume a uniformity of nature because they perceive and act in accordance with the law of cause and effect. They also have a memory, which means they have a subconscious. Their minds did not create any of this. Their minds do not distort their awareness of reality. Each species does have a distinctive form of consciousness, just as humans have their distinctive form, but the function of consciousness in the higher animals and humans alike is to be conscious of existence.[13]

The key word here is "form" of awareness, as opposed to its object. Each species has its own form of awareness.[14] Dogs, for example, have limited color vision because they have only two types of cones, as do red-green color blind humans.[15] The object of their perception, however, is still there and that is what they perceive, the same thing that we perceive. Flies, with their compound eyes, see at best a mosaic of the world, but it is still the world that they are perceiving. This form-object distinction also applies to our consciousness. Humans have a specific form of consciousness, just as other animals do, but ours is more advanced than the higher animals. We can form universal concepts and write scientific treatises.

---

[13]"The problem of how a mind can know an external world," says John Dewey, "or even know that there is such a thing is like the problem of how an animal eats things external to itself." John Dewey, *Experience and Nature*, 2nd ed. (Chicago: Open Court, 1929), 227. To state the so-called problem of the external world, says Dewey, is to assume the world's existence and a knowledge of it. To deny "true reality" or our ability to know it is self-contradictory.

[14]On the form-object distinction, see Rand, *Objectivist Epistemology*, 281.

[15]Dogs perceive color, not just black and white. Joseph Stromberg, "New Study Shows That Dogs Use Color Vision After All," *Smithsonian.com*, July 17, 2013, https://www.smithsonianmag.com/. Search article title.

The form of our consciousness, its essential distinguishing characteristic, is its rational faculty, which is what enables us to accumulate knowledge far beyond what the higher animals are capable of. Because we (and the higher animals, for that matter) can only hold a small amount of the knowledge in our conscious awareness at any one time, most of it is held subconsciously. Some of that knowledge is retrievable at will, some with effort. This last includes material that has been repressed, though much of it is still there and with the right technique can be retrieved.

It is this stored knowledge, which includes our core and mid-level evaluations from childhood and adolescence, that influences our present perceptions and behavior. It is this stored knowledge, because everyone's is different, that leads to the Kantian conclusion that we cannot correctly perceive reality. All it means, however, is that we each have different perspectives on the world, based on our different stored knowledge, different cognitive capabilities, and different choices of what to focus on. What we need to learn is how to introspect and apply logic to the contents and processes of the consciousness that we do possess. This will then determine correct or incorrect identification of reality. If we can perceive reality, we can perceive facts, which means we can become independent.

Kant is wrong. Reality is there, accessible to our consciousness, and independent judgment and action are possible.

THE TWO AUTONOMIES

A concept frequently associated with and sometimes said to be a synonym of independence is autonomy. However, there are two meanings of the term, the first deriving from the philosophy of Kant, the second from the philosophy of individualism.

Self-Determination as Voluntary Self-Sacrifice

"In Kantian philosophy," says the *Oxford English Dictionary*, autonomy is "the freedom of will which enables a person to adopt the rational principles of moral law (rather than personal desire or feeling) as the prerequisite for his or her actions; the capacity of reason for moral self-determination."[16]

Although this definition may sound lofty, self-determining, and individualistic, its key phrase is "rather than personal desire or feeling." Kant's concept of autonomy is based on his ethics, the categorical imperatives, the most fundamental one being that we should all act from duty, not inclination. Duty means obedience to a higher authority without regard for personal consequence; in Kant's case the higher authority, although he claims to have defined a secular morality based on reason, is the Christian God. The OED's definition says "rational principles of moral law," but those principles derive ultimately from Kant's "noumenal" world of the higher being. Duty means to act in such a way as to respect, obey, and defer to a superior power regardless of whether one receives any benefit or joy or pleasure in return. This is the meaning of not acting from inclination. Acting to gain benefit or pleasure or to feel good or better about ourselves would be selfish.[17]

Kant's concept of autonomy means that we should act in a freely chosen and uncoerced way to fulfill our duty to the higher authority. "Freely chosen and uncoerced" means no one has to ask us to act in this way or force us to do it. This is what Kant means by "self-determination." Those who must be asked or made to act are less moral than those who have the "will power"—free of external influence—to act completely without or against personal desire or pleasure. This is the essence of self-sacrifice, in the sense of giving up a higher value for the sake of a lower- or non-value. In the practical sense, on earth, it means placing the interest of others above our own self-interest. Kant's concept of autonomy is based entirely on the doctrine of altruism that provides the foundation of collectivism.

---

[16] *Oxford English Dictionary Online*, s.v. "autonomy," accessed February 8, 2019, http://www.oed.com.

[17] In contrast to duty, obligation is a chosen commitment, such as a contract or promise. See Ayn Rand's discussion of duty as an "anti-concept," "Causality Versus Duty," in *Philosophy: Who needs It*, 114–22.

Psychologist Edward Deci endorses autonomy as an admirable virtue of self-determination, but differentiates it from individualism and independence.[18] Indeed, he goes to great lengths to demonstrate how autonomy, on the one hand, and individualism and independence, on the other—all narrowly construed—are not causally related; they are "orthogonal" (that is, separate and distinct from one another), to quote his statistical jargon, although they can occur together under certain circumstances. Beneath the verbiage and pretensions to sophisticated research, Deci is using the Kantian version of autonomy.

For Deci, autonomy "means to act freely, with a sense of volition and choice," while independence "means to do for yourself, to *not* rely on others for personal nourishment and emotional support." Independent people, he says, often are driven and controlled, either by "inner or outer forces"; they do not act by choice.[19] Individualism is defined somewhat correctly, in that he says it is based on individual rights and that the individualistic person is "free to pursue [his or her] own ends." He goes on to say, however, that individualism is not concerned with the "common good."[20] Most business people, who are his models of individualism, are said to be controlled by the compulsion to achieve and, therefore, are not free or autonomous.[21]

---

[18]Edward L. Deci and Richard Flaste, *Why We Do What We Do: Understanding Self-Motivation* (New York: Penguin Books, 1995). This book is an accessible summary of Deci's extensive research on autonomy and intrinsic motivation. I refer mainly to it though the following article provides further distinction (by Deci colleagues and students) between autonomy, on the one hand, and individualism and independence, on the other: Valery Chirkov et al., "Differentiating Autonomy From Individualism and Independence: A Self-Determination Theory Perspective on Internalization of Cultural Orientations and Well-Being," *Journal of Personality and Social Psychology* 84, no. 1 (2003), 97–110.

[19]Deci and Flaste, *Why We Do What We Do*, 89 (Deci's italics).

[20]Deci and Flaste, *Why We Do What We Do*, 134. "Common good," of course, is the catchphrase that allegedly means everyone benefits, though in practice it means what the ruling elites define as "common good." Deci intends, falsely, that individualism cannot and does not benefit everyone.

[21]An underlying motif of Deci's work and all Kantian and collectivist notions of independence and egoism is that independent judgment is fundamentally subjectivist, meaning "because I made the choice, I am independent." This is

Deci is trying to distinguish the three concepts by saying that the independent person can be autonomous, but often is not, as the individualistic person can be autonomous, or not. He even states that collectivists can be autonomous, or not, depending on how freely chosen and self-determining their actions are. All of these terms, as often occurs in psychological research today, are examples of fuzzy definition by nonessentials. And as in the superficiality of research on repression, they stem from the shoehorning requirements of the "experimental-positivistic-behavioristic" epistemology.

The lack of philosophical sophistication and understanding of the concepts involved leads to substantial muddiness in what Deci is claiming to accomplish. His obvious goal is to praise autonomy while rejecting individualism, independence, and capitalism.[22] By saying that "individualism stands in contrast to acting for the common good," Deci gives away his basic premise, namely that individualism and "anarchic" capitalism do not and cannot work for the increased wealth and happiness of all, yet this is precisely what Adam Smith's invisible hand means.[23] In addition, Deci critiques the "greed" decade of the 1980s, which supposedly was the decade of egoism, individualism, and capitalism. For Deci, it was a decade that lacked autonomy and authenticity and his Kantian higher authority is apparently society and the common good. This is consistent with the collectivist principles of the early and current Progressives.

The Kantian concept of autonomy means *voluntarily* sacrificing ourselves either to God or to society.

counterfeit egoism, counterfeit individualism, and counterfeit independence. As Ayn Rand says, "Only reference to a demonstrable principle can validate one's choices," which means based on *objective, rational* evidence. Rand, "Introduction," in *Virtue of Selfishness*, xiv. See also Branden, *Psychology of Self-Esteem*, 189–91.

[22] A rarity in contemporary research literature is Deci's mention of Ayn Rand as a representative of individualism and capitalism, but he does not do so approvingly. Deci and Flaste, *Why We Do What We Do*, 133, 208.

[23] "Anarchic" is my word, typically used by opponents of capitalism, as in the "unplanned anarchy of the marketplace." Deci does not use the word, though it is implied.

Self-Determination as Voluntary Pursuit of Self-Interest

Deci hints at a proper understanding of autonomy when he states that independent people are often driven or controlled by "inner or outer forces," his implication, apparently, that autonomy means *not* being so driven or controlled. This understanding of autonomy also seems to be the thrust of most psychotherapists working in the humanistic tradition; that is, they focus on the removal of internal inhibitions and provide an understanding of how better to deal with and minimize external controls. When Deci, however, restricts independence to not relying "on others for personal nourishment and emotional support" and relegates individualism to a self-centered compulsion to achieve that fails to benefit others, he reveals a shallow and conventional understanding of the concepts.

The Greek root of autonomy is *autonomia* or *autonomos* and it means "living by one's own laws" or "independence," referring generally to the city-state.[24] Although the ancient Greeks were egoists, and not advocates of self-sacrifice, they do not seem to have applied *autonomia* (or *autonomos*) to themselves as individuals. Modern usage has taken the political term and narrowed it to each one of us. Hence, autonomy today has come to mean self-determination or self-rule, not just of our city-state or country, but also of each one of us. Heteronomy is the opposite and means subjection or subordination to others, which is another name for dependence, whether in politics or morality and psychology. The point here is that a correct understanding of autonomy recognizes that its origin and development has little to do with self-sacrifice and a lot to do with independence.

A formal definition of autonomy would say that it is a psychology of choosing values and acting on them based on one's own first-hand, objective perception of reality. As a positive cognitive and behavioral action, it means seeing what one sees and doing what one judges best to do. As a negative, it means seeing and acting without the interference of (internal) defensive habits and (external) environmental constraints.

---

[24] *A Lexicon: Abridged from Liddell and Scott's Greek-English Lexicon* (Oxford: Oxford University Press: 1963), s.v. "autonomia," "autonomos."

The absence of defensive habits means a healthy psychology and the absence of external control means a free society. Typical usage puts emphasis on the behavioral component, that is, acting without internal or external interference, giving us the short-hand versions of autonomy as self-determination or self-regulation. Autonomy is essentially the same concept as psychological independence, but the former emphasizes self-rule of one's behavior, while the latter emphasizes self-rule of one's consciousness.

Our personalities are self-created, because we must process all data that enters our minds, then generate the beliefs and values that motivate us to act in certain ways. But a self-created personality is not automatically an egoistic or self-interested one. That is the fallacy of psychological egoism. We do not, by nature, automatically act for the sake of our own, objectively selfish welfare. There are too many self-destructive people in the world to believe that everyone is egoistic. The psychotherapy profession spends hours and months helping self-destructive people correct their thinking errors by giving them the strength and knowledge to become more self-determined and self-ruled. Most unhappy personalities are precisely those who have failed to develop into autonomously self-interested individuals.[25]

True (individualistic) autonomy is the voluntary pursuit of one's own objective self-interest, neither sacrificing oneself to others nor others to oneself. The pursuit of objective self-interest is action to meet the demonstrably correct requirements of life and happiness. Such action produces individuals with strong personal identities who take responsibility for their lives. These requirements are the same ones necessary to create and sustain a free society.

THE TWO RESPONSIBILITIES

Independence requires a strong personal identity and commitment to self-responsibility. As with autonomy, there are two conceptions of independence: sound judgment or wisdom, which can be described as

---

[25] Szasz saw the goal of therapy as "preservation and expansion of the patient's autonomy." Szasz, *Ethics of Psychoanalysis*, 7.

taking existential responsibility for one's life, and independent judgment and action, or true independence, which requires the commitment of also taking psychological responsibility.

Existential responsibility focuses on externals, which means paying one's bills so as in adulthood not to be dependent financially on others, especially one's parents. It means in addition making reasoned, not impulsive or reckless, life decisions in one's choice of career, friends, and spouse. It means sound, not necessarily independent, judgment. Sound judgment and its synonyms—wisdom, sagacity, prudence—mean rational or sensible decision making. Of people exhibiting these traits, we would likely say, "They have their acts together. They know what they want and are on their way to achieving their goals. We admire their independence." Or if already successful, we would say, "These people have accomplished so much. They're highly independent."

Such people are existentially responsible and practice sound judgment. Existential responsibility and sound judgment is what most parents would like to see in their children as adults and this also is the aim of most educators. I do not mean to take anything away from those who exhibit sound judgment. It is an accomplishment worthy of admiration, but it is not true independence. Accumulated knowledge, assorted chosen values and skills, and, of course, money and other material riches do not give one independent judgment, and observing these values and accomplishments in others does not entitle us to conclude that such people are truly independent. Judging by externals, meaning what people say and do, can give clues to another's psychology, but getting to know others personally and closely is the only way to begin to understand them.

Further, judging another person by surface appearances can be risky. People who say they are happy are not necessarily so.[26] And people who say they are independent, and exhibit certain traits and behaviors that

---

[26] It is especially risky to judge a friend or relative as happy when such a person has been seriously depressed for some time and suddenly shows a positive change of mood. This can be a danger signal that the depressive has decided to take his or her life.

look like independence, may just be role playing, which is a defensive habit. What people say and do may not be who they are deep down. Dependent personalities are sometimes good at parroting the words and imitating the behavior of independent people, but inside they may be riveted with anxiety and insecurity. This is something that psychotherapists can readily confirm, as well as confidential friends. [27]

Sometimes, there are external words and behaviors that do indicate independence or dependence. The boy in the story of the Emperor's New Clothes and the reaction of the adults is a simple example of both. In literature we have the independent personality of Dr. Thomas Stockmann in Henrik Ibsen's play *An Enemy of the People* and the fearful followers of the crowd, the "compact majority," who, one by one, claimed to be his friend but deserted him. [28] And of course, we have Howard Roark, the independent hero of Ayn Rand's *The Fountainhead* and the very dependent Peter Keating, plus other characters, dependent in varying degrees, who oppose Roark. Interestingly, many of the dependent characters who oppose the independent heroes in these two stories would be considered independent in the conventional, existential sense. Exercising independent judgment and action, however, they do not do.

In life, true innovators who challenge the conventional wisdom of their fields, by definition, are independent, at least in their work. This includes Socrates and Galileo. On the other hand, politicians are

---

[27] Note a parallel here to criminal personalities many of whom are professional con artists, expert at imitating the life of a responsible citizen. Most dependent personalities, of course, are not con artists or criminals, but criminal personalities are decidedly dependent, several notches worse than the law-abiding dependent person. Difficulty in judging someone without knowing that person well is the flaw in conventional self-report questionnaires. No matter how carefully a "measuring instrument" may be structured and worded, there is no guarantee that it is discovering what it is claiming to discover, that is, is valid. It is not a *conceptualizing process*, which only a therapist or confidential friend can perform.

[28] Needless to say, I do not endorse contemporary interpretations of the play as championing the pseudo issue of environment versus business, nor do I support— nor did Ibsen—any form of political elitism or aristocracy of birth. Arthur Miller quotes Ibsen: "Of course I do not mean the aristocracy of birth, or of the purse, or even the aristocracy of the intellect. I mean the aristocracy of character, of will, of mind—that alone can free us." *Arthur Miller's Adaptation of "An Enemy of the People" by Henrik Ibsen* (New York: Viking Penguin, 1951), 10.

known as expert compromisers, not just on particulars that are morally optional, but most dishearteningly on serious abstract principles. Neville Chamberlain, Prime Minister of the United Kingdom, is frequently associated with the word "appeasement" for his 1938 agreement to allow Hitler to march unchallenged into the Sudetenland. The deal with a brazen and vicious aggressor was supposed to promise "peace in our time," which it did not achieve.[29]

What we do not know about these contrarians and compromisers, both in fiction and in real life, is what is going on in their minds, and has been going on since childhood. In particular, we do not know their core and mid-level evaluations. What few early concrete events that fiction writers and biographers give us may enable us to infer parts of their psychology, but reading plays, novels, and biographies is equivalent to a real-life *casual* relationship. We do not in fact know what deep down makes them tick, or rather, what is the origin and development of their psychologies.[30]

Not that we have a right to know what a stranger's or casual friend's core and mid-level evaluations are, unless they volunteer them. Probing or speculating about another person's psychology, especially when the other person is dead or, if alive, when we do not know the other person, or know the person well, is the fallacy of psychologizing. From the standpoint of the science of psychology, however, which includes parenting and education, it would advance the field to conceptualize core and mid-level evaluations of highly independent people, both famous and not so famous, identifying choice points and methods of using their minds that led to their development. Much literature exists on the less than healthy personalities, little on the independent ones.[31]

---

[29]Politicians and other people who claim to be oh-so-independent are usually just posturers.

[30]I include here the characters in Ayn Rand's novels. Some events from childhood are described, but many conclusions the characters have drawn about themselves, others, and the world, especially as related to the early events and parental relationships of their childhoods, are missing.

[31]This was Maslow's complaint, that psychology spends too much time on pathology, not enough on health. Maslow's studies of self-actualizers are a rare exception. Maslow, *Psychology of Being*, 14–18. My call is for research on

Some advocates of sensible decision making may claim that Socrates, Galileo, and Stockmann, by stirring the hornet's nests in which they lived, caused their own headaches by not being reasonable. But there are two issues here. Are the advocates of sensible decision making saying that these three men should have given up their independent judgments in order to conform to the majority? If so, that is a dependent personality talking. Or, are they bringing up the Socrates issue by saying that independent judgment does not require sacrifices when under duress?

The rational principle of self-defense indeed does say that self-sacrifice is not required in these cases, that is, that it is morally equivalent to fight, flee, or put on a pretense of agreement when threatened with force. Socrates and Stockmann refused to flee, so Socrates died, which as I argue above he did not have to do, but Stockmann in Roark-like fashion stood his ground and remained to fight. Galileo took the third path of appearing to give in by recanting, but to himself maintained his independence. Abject conformity or sacrificing one's independent judgment was not considered by any of these men. The issue when confronted with coercion is one of practicality: is it safe to fight or flee, or should I put on a front?

INDEPENDENCE AND INTELLIGENCE

A free society requires rebels—people like Socrates, Galileo, and Thomas Stockmann whose independence leads them to see and say what the majority cannot. People with independent judgment are the innovators and entrepreneurs who move economies and societies forward. They rock boats, not necessarily on purpose, but because they see things others do not. Does this not mean that only the highly intelligent can consistently practice independence, whereas the rest of us must resign ourselves to sound judgment and existential responsibility?

Independent judgment is the willed choice to perceive reality uncontaminated by one's unexamined or out-of-context emotions or

---

early evaluations of the psychologically independent, not just self-actualizers or the existentially independent.

by false opinions of others. This perception is then followed by the willed choice to act on what was perceived. Where does intelligence fit in? Intelligence is a capacity or ability, not a choice or issue of will power, as is independence. Anyone with a normal brain at any intelligence level can practice true independence.

As the *Oxford English Dictionary* defines it, intelligence is "quickness or superiority of understanding," or the "quick wit" to put it in the vernacular.[32] It means making connections and grasping an insight before others. It may involve, as Ayn Rand has stated, "the ability to deal with a broad range of abstractions" and "to deal with them long-range," but, I submit, this is not the essential distinguishing characteristic of intelligence.[33] Conceptual thought, and this includes independent judgment, is not a monopoly of the highly educated or intelligent. Conversations with skilled and unskilled laborers, if one is paying attention to what they are saying, can indicate the presence of an intelligence, albeit one lacking accumulated knowledge or skill in using broad abstractions and long-range thinking, although even these may be present in the laborers' areas of work.

There is an analogy between intelligence and independence in the sense that both are a perception and both require action based on the perception. In business, for example, many of us may see a profit-making opportunity in the marketplace, but fail to take advantage of it for many reasons. We may lack knowledge of how to execute the idea, have no desire to act, or if rocking the boat is involved, may fear opposition due to our issues of dependence. Innovative entrepreneurs are both intelligent and independent because they see and seize profit-making opportunities, and often gladly go forth to rock the boat. That is, they readily perceive the opportunities, then act on their perceptions.

Knowledge and desire, however, are two concepts worthy of discussion in parsing the relationship between intelligence and independence.

---

[32] *Oxford English Dictionary Online*, s.v. "intelligence," accessed February 8, 2019, http://www.oed.com.

[33] Ayn Rand, "The Comprachicos," in *The New Left: The Anti-Industrial Revolution* (New York: Signet, 1975), 195, and Rand, "Metaphysical Versus the Man-Made," 40.

Innovative scientists and entrepreneurs both possess a huge context of knowledge that they have built up over the course of their careers. They also are both highly interested in, that is, motivated by, their areas of work and have been so in most cases from an early age. The huge context of knowledge and strong interest are not irrelevant in the "quick wit" of intelligent people. Knowledge and desire to a great degree is what enables them to see ahead of others what we would likely call a stroke of genius. Their motivation—knowledge and desire built up over time—tends also to encourage an attitude of not caring about ruffled feathers.

Is this combination of intelligence and independence that we see in geniuses inborn? Or is it a result of accumulated knowledge, interest, and *chosen* concentrated attention? These questions are worthy of further study via the conceptualization process, by looking at early childhood experiences of such people, especially their core and mid-level evaluations, with an eye on the role of free will in their development. The "experimental-positivistic-behavioristic" methodology would not be able to handle the assignment, and it certainly would not allow such a term as "free will" into the discussion.[34]

Yes, knowledge, or a context of subject matter, is required to make great accomplishments and great discoveries possible, but I am convinced that anyone with a normal brain, a good teacher, and patience can learn that context of knowledge, however abstract it may be. Interest and will power, if present, can take such a student to the next level.

Quality of education is key, but this also includes an education in introspective competence.

---

[34]Conceptualization does occur in "experimental-positivistic-behavioristic" studies, a myriad of which I had to read in graduate school and today still occasionally peruse, but it usually occurs in the sections labeled "literature review" and "summary and conclusions." The study itself and the "vast wasteland" (to borrow Newton Minnow's 1961 phrase about television) of statistical analysis is largely useless and, as has been complained about in recent years, difficult to replicate. Why so difficult to replicate? The fundamental reason, never mind questionable methodological practices, is that the subject under study in the human sciences possesses free will, and unless that is explicitly taken into account before beginning a project, humans can change their minds and destroy the best research design. Astute observers and reporters, like Freud and Jane Goodall, not statisticians, are needed in the so-called softer sciences.

INDEPENDENCE AND CERTAINTY

In our current age of post-Kantian skepticism and relativism, it follows, according to the skeptics and relativists, that anyone claiming epistemological or ethical certainty is either a deluded fundamentalist or a wannabe or actual dictator.[35]

Inquisitors and jihadis are certain of their convictions and maim and kill those who do not agree with them. Hitler was certain and viciously imposed his will on his own citizens and the world and, of course, the Jewish people. The implication is that inquisitors, jihadis, and Hitlers are selfish, independent personalities. The argument often does not go this far, though it is implied, and some, including Holocaust scholars, have said as much.[36] After all, this train of thought continues, no one is omniscient and because of our inherent fallibility, we must allow freedom of speech. This is what makes a society free. Lack of omniscience means inability to be certain, which means we must invite and relish criticism to clarify our thoughts, and perhaps gradually get closer and closer to the truth, though absolute truth can never be attained. This is what logical positivism and its offspring have taught us. Claims of certainty are dangerous. We have to talk things over and aim for consensus, sometimes through voting. This in essence is the epistemological justification of democracy.[37]

In other words, according to this line of thought anyone who believes in absolutes believes in absolute authority. The independent personality is one who asserts facts as absolutely true, and that is what is dangerous.

So does this mean the boy in the story of the Emperor's New Clothes should request a vote before speaking up (assuming the Socrates issue is

---

[35] Some educators have even called the lecture method of teaching "coercive" and "dictatorial," and apparently mean the words literally, not metaphorically.

[36] I heard philosopher John K. Roth, in the question period of a lecture given at my university, associate certainty with the Nazis. Epistemological agnosticism and skepticism, he said, was safer and less authoritarian for a free society.

[37] The argument is John Stuart Mill's utilitarian defense of free speech, restated in Jonathan Rauch, *Kindly Inquisitors: The New Attacks on Free Thought* (Chicago: University of Chicago Press, 1993). Rauch in 1993 was responding to an early wave of censorship by political correctness.

not present)? In addition to their self-contradictions, this is one *reductio ad absurdum* of skepticism and relativism.[38]

It does not follow from human fallibility that absolute certainty is authoritarian or that strong, independent personalities are actual or wannabe dictators. Nor is the argument from fallibility the actual or fundamental defense of freedom of speech and the free society.

In a single sentence, the answer to this issue is a sound, objective theory of universals that allows the identification of sound, objective values, which in turn defines social relationships in terms of individual rights, that is, freedoms to act without being coerced, including the freedom to express oneself on one's own property or on that of someone else with whom one has contracted to make that expression. Freedom of speech presupposes property rights, and democracy, if it is not to be a form of dictatorship, presupposes and is restrained by all individual rights, which therefore means democracy in a free society is demoted to the relatively minor function of defining procedures and selecting leaders. Democracy is not the arbiter of truth (or "approximate" truth) or of ethical or legal behavior.

The sound theory of universals is Ayn Rand's.[39] It is a theory based on the contextual nature of knowledge that allows certainty to be asserted of an absolute truth within a specified context. Because knowledge grows over time, adjustments to earlier absolute certainties may have to be made, as Newton's theories were adjusted by Einstein's. Yet, something over the years must have been right, true, and certain about Newton's and Einstein's ideas, because in the use of both theories, spaceships have gone to the moon and back. Truth and certainty—by peaceful, independent-minded, non-authoritarian scientists—do seem possible.

---

[38] Here are the self-contradictions: skeptics assert as an absolute certainty that certainty is impossible and relativists claim absolutely that all claims are relative. Cratylus, the Greek skeptic who stopped talking, is another reductio. In the two-word phrase "absolute certainty," the word "absolute" is redundant. Knowledge is certain absolutely in a given state or context of knowledge. As knowledge grows, the new context is certain . . . absolutely.

[39] Rand, *Objectivist Epistemology*, throughout.

Yes, we are fallible and not omniscient, which means we must submit our expressions to evaluation and criticism and be prepared to defend them, but this is not a justification of freedom of speech. In order to survive and flourish, humans must exercise their inborn, volitional capacity to reason. Because this exercise of reason is not activated by our genes or environment, we must be left free to choose—that is, it is right or moral for us to be free from the coercion of others, especially the government—to allow each of us as individuals to generate and sustain action to achieve our chosen values. Trade is our means of social cooperation. The source and justification of individual rights is our nature as rational beings. It is right and moral to be free of any initiation against us of the use of physical force.

Thus, whatever we say or write, either on our own property or on that of the others cooperating with us, is, at least sometimes, an assertion of truth and certainty. It is right and moral for us to make these assertions, first, because our freedom of expression is consonant with and required by our human nature and, second, because our speech, writing, and expressions derive from our rights to life, liberty and property.

Inquisitors, jihadis, and Hitlers of the world, in contrast, do also make assertions of truth and certainty, but they back up their assertions with a gun. Their expressions are not open to evaluation and criticism because they tolerate no disagreement. They are the authoritarians, the dictators who at root, as Stanton Samenow explains, are criminal personalities. As liars and cheaters, they are not the least bit interested in perceiving and asserting facts as facts. They most certainly are not independent personalities; they are among the worst of the dependent.[40] Brandishing and using guns, as they do, is anathema to our rational nature. Their goals and accomplishments are to silence reason. Their "truth" and "certainty" lead to wanton destruction of humankind and civilization.

Talking and voting does not make any individual more or less independent, and it is not the means of preventing another Holocaust. Lack

---

[40] Samenow, *Inside the Criminal Mind*, chap. 10.

of certainty may indicate insecurity or insufficient knowledge to make a decision with confidence. To link certainty to dictatorship is the red herring of all red herrings, brought to us by post-Kantian agnosticism, both in epistemology and ethics. It is time to restore certainty to its proper place in knowledge and values, and in the free society.

THE DEFERENCE TO AUTHORITY STUDIES

Independent judgment should be a fundamental aim of parenting and teaching.

Independence means that one's psychological disposition, that is, one's self-esteem, integrity, and courage, should be sufficiently strong to resist outside pressures for conformity. Instilling this trait in children and students is a large order for both parents and teachers to fill, and will be addressed in the next chapter. For now, a number of studies that have examined, albeit superficially, the relationship between independence and conformity should be mentioned.

Solomon Asch explicitly approached the issue in terms of independence versus conformity, and he even referred to Ibsen's "compact majority." His studies exposed a group of subjects to four straight lines on a card. The group's assignment was to judge which of three lines was equal in length to the fourth; only one of the three was equal. All but one subject were confederates of the researchers and were instructed to give identically *in*correct answers. The test was to determine how independent the lone, unaware subject would be against the pressures of the group. Several trials with variations were also conducted.[41]

On average, two-thirds of all naïve subjects, in at least one of several trials, did not conform to the majority. Twenty-five percent did not conform at all in any trial. What does this prove? Not much. It does show the serious shortcomings, especially the contrived nature and shallowness, of the experimental-positivistic-behavioristic epistemology. The

---

[41]S. E. Asch, "Effects of Group Pressure upon the Modification and Distortion of Judgments," in *Readings in Social Psychology* (New York: Henry Holt, 1952), 7. Asch, "Studies of Independence and Conformity," *Psychological Monographs: General and Applied* 70, no. 9 (1956), 1–70.

studies only establish that some people are independent and others are not, though, as Asch points out, there are "individual differences" in the behavior of all personalities. Follow-up interviews provided some, but not much, insight into the thinking of test subjects. And because of the absence of any further probing into the thinking, especially of the core and mid-level evaluations of subjects, the concept of independence used must be described as existential, not psychological.

Similarly, subsequent studies showed the same results, namely that some people are independent and others are not, and that the shallowness of the methods used provided no in-depth understanding of the participants' psychologies. Stanley Milgram's obedience-to-authority studies, under a pretext of being studies of learning, asked "teachers" to repeatedly increase the voltage of electrical shocks to a "learner" (who was a confederate of the researcher). The shocks were not real, but the teachers did not know it.[42] Philip Zimbardo's 1971 Stanford Prison Experiment divided students into "prisoners" and "guards" in a mock prison situation for several days. Realistic submissiveness and depression of the "prisoners" and aggression and sadism of the "guards" caused the intended two-week experiment to be shut down after six days.[43]

---

[42] Stanley Milgram, *Obedience to Authority: An Experimental View* (New York: Harper Perennial, 1975). Milgram refers to his studies as research on "obedience to authority," but historian Christopher Browning says obedience means compliance with commands, whereas deference is the more correct term because deference means submission to superior claims—of the researcher, in the case of Milgram's studies, and others. The "deference to authority" studies are not Nazi-style situations of obedience backed up with a gun pointed at you. Consequently, agreeing with Browning, I have used "deference" in the title of this section. Christopher R. Browning, "Revisiting the Holocaust Perpetrators: Why Did They Kill?" (lecture, University of North Carolina, Chapel Hill, NC, October 17, 2011. https://bhecinfo.org/wp-content/uploads/Revisiting-the-Holocaust-Perpetrators_Why-Did-They-Kill.pdf.). Why did the perpetrators kill? First, they dehumanized the victims, then followed the crowd. Independence, if ever present, was jettisoned, though some in at least one battalion were allowed to opt out by their commanding officer. Others who had no choice would misfire, aiming above or to the side of the victims. Even in the Holocaust, some were independent, some were not.

[43] Philip Zimbardo, *The Lucifer Effect: Understanding How Good People Turn Evil* (New York: Random House, 2007).

These studies may be interesting to read, but they still only confirm the obvious, namely that some people are independent and others are not.[44] They provide data about how different people may behave in different situations, but that is all. Not everyone increased the voltages in Milgram's studies, and not every prisoner in Zimbardo's study was submissive or depressed, nor was every guard aggressive or sadistic. Psychologies differ—and it matters. Psychologies were hardly examined. This reveals the fundamental flaw in positivism and its so-called scientific methodology, especially as it is applied in the human sciences.

Every subject in these studies is viewed not as an individual exhibiting universal traits, universal core and mid-level evaluations, or various levels of self-esteem, but as a member—a single unit—of a statistical group that enables the researchers to calculate averages and percentages, and to compare the subjects to hundreds and thousands of others before "projection by successive approximation" can be made. Viewing people as members of a statistical group in order to calculate averages and percentages and make projections strips them of their individuality and collectivizes them. At the same time, it abdicates the scientific search for universals, the search for answers to such questions as, "Why do some people go along with the group and others do not?" The essence and assumption of positivism (or should I say, citing the self-excepting fallacy, the *universal* essence and assumption?) is the Kantian inability to know or identify universals.

The deference to authority studies were motivated in part by a desire to understand the Holocaust of World War II, to understand, for example, why some people would hide and protect an Anne Frank, others would tolerate the hiding but not do it themselves, and still others would inform on the protectors. A clue comes not from one-dimensionally descriptive surveys or ostensibly causal studies, but from the scientific observation of Victor Frankl. As a concentration camp prisoner, Frankl observed with his eyes and through communication with his fellow inmates. Although he did not use the term, self-esteem was

---

[44]Interesting sometimes to read as history, to use the distinction between theory and history of Ludwig von Mises. Theory, these studies are not.

what enabled prisoners of "less hardy make-up . . . to survive camp life better than did those of a robust nature." A "life of inner riches and spiritual freedom" is how Frankl put it. Self-esteem, integrity, courage, and independence are what give us that inner strength—to withstand evil or to go against a "compact majority."[45]

In our final chapter we will now explore the task of teaching the character and personality traits of independence and independent judgment. The ultimate aim is that parents and teachers learn the skill of introspection and pass on to their children and students the skills both of introspection and independent judgment. For both are skills that can be learned, as well as applied, though not easily the older one gets, to one's life. The aim of all education, whether parental, formal, or lifelong, should be the development and practice of introspection and independent judgment. Both are necessary for individual health and happiness—and for the survival of free societies.

---

[45] Victor Frankl, *Man's Search for Meaning* (Boston: Beacon Press, 1959), 36.

5
Educating for Independence

The crucial task is to educate parents to bring up children who are able to develop correct attitudes and who are equipped to deal with reality, whatever the circumstances. This can be accomplished only by understanding the process of how the child reacts to his experiences and what conclusions he draws from them. By helping him to avoid mistakes in evaluating his experiences and by being on hand to clarify and correct his thinking, parents can be instrumental in helping their child to form correct core evaluations.

—Edith Packer[1]

THE GOAL OF PARENTING AND TEACHING in a free society is, or should be, to prepare the young for adult life as independently thinking human beings.

Ideally, the individual of independent judgment would possess high self-esteem, a positive and benevolent outlook on life, and, most fundamentally, a keen skill in introspection to prevent the development of significant inhibitions to mental health and happiness that may arise and, if the inhibitions do arise, the skill to identify and remove them. This skill is the required means to the end of a strong personal identity and a strong sense of psychological responsibility. Acquisition of the skill must begin at an early age, the earlier the better. And parents and teachers themselves must be skilled in introspection in order to

---

[1]Packer, "Understanding the Subconscious," 25.

teach it to their charges, a preventive maintenance, as it were, of their children's conscious and subconscious minds, which includes a collection of techniques for identifying and correcting problems.

The task is one of education—of both adults and children—about psychology and introspection. Edith Packer comments:

> If it were up to me, I would recommend that anxiety, mental health, and emotions all be taught, starting with kindergarten and the first grade. Few people would need therapy if that were done. If parents and schools could teach children the connection between thoughts and emotions, if they could teach a child that when he feels something, he's really thinking something—so that the child would learn to ask himself, 'What am I thinking when I experience this emotion?'—it would be invaluable.[2]

There is nothing automatic about child-rearing or teaching. Our tendency throughout history has been to repeat, with minimal change, what our parents and teachers did as parents and teachers, who in turn repeated what their parents and teachers did as parents and teachers, and so on. To avoid this infinitely regressive cycle, adults must rise above their own upbringings and youthful classrooms. They must learn new skills—psychological skills—of child-rearing and teaching, but learning these new skills is not easy.

It is to the skills of independence that we now turn.

THE MEANING OF INTROSPECTION

Extrospection is observation, direct perception and conclusions based on those perceptions, of everything outside our minds, which includes our bodies, other people, and the universe. Introspection is observation, direct perception and conclusions based on those perceptions, of the content and processes of our own minds. Processes include thinking, evaluating, feeling, and remembering, while the content includes products of the processes: thoughts and knowledge, values, emotions, memories. Mental content derives ultimately from our awareness of the external world, as extrospection is the foundation

---

[2] Edith Packer, "An Interview with Edith Packer on Psychotherapy," in *Lectures on Psychology*, 278.

on which introspection rests. Logic is the tool by which we assess the accuracy of our conclusions, that is, the extent to which our extrospections correctly identify the external world and our introspections correctly identify our internal world, including the mental requirements of both internal and external awareness. Introspection identifies the proper methods of using our minds.

There are healthy methods of using our minds that contribute to the achievement of happiness and there are unhealthy methods that produce anxiety and defensive maneuvers and, ultimately, unhappiness. For example, perceiving the facts as facts and asserting them despite disagreement and disapproval of others is a sound method of using our minds. Succumbing to fear of disagreement and disapproval, or worse, failing to perceive the facts correctly because of the policy of acting blindly on emotion, rather than following all relevant evidence, is an unsound method. Introspection to be aware of either method, as well as all other methods that we may use, is prerequisite to understanding our psychologies and correcting what we find. Introspection is what we use to identify the nature and cause of our emotions, as well as our core and mid-level evaluations.

What introspection is not, according to Packer, is what she calls "continuous defensive observation." This is a superficial looking inward that seeks to answer the question, "How am I doing?" in relation to other people. It is a dependent, self-conscious focus on what others may think of us. It is usually driven by fear or anxiety, which makes it an unhealthy method of using our minds. Healthy introspection seeks answers to the questions, "What am I doing and why am I doing it?"[3]

CORE EVALUATION IN THE MAKING

One of the most important areas in which we must learn to introspect—and in which parents and teachers must learn to assist their children and students—is in the discovery and correction of mistaken core evaluations.

---

[3]Packer, "Art of Introspection," 222.

Packer relates this story of a mother and her six-year-old son. The boy stopped wanting to go to school and even cried at the prospect.[4] When the mother, worried that her son was developing a phobia of school, began to question him, she learned that he felt he had no friends because no one liked him. Upon further questioning, the mother discovered that her son had asked his classmates to play with him and his toy soldiers. It turned out that no one wanted to play with toy soldiers, so the mother patiently explained that that did not mean his classmates did not like him. Rather, it likely meant that they did not want to play with the soldiers, and she emphasized that that was also true of her friends who sometimes do not like the same things as she does. Her friends still like her.

The boy stopped crying and went back to school. Packer calls this story a "core evaluation in the making" because it illustrates the beginnings of a conclusion, a mistaken one, about other people and their relation to the boy. Repeated many times, that is, concluding that "people don't like me," in many similar concrete situations is what eventually leads to a hardened and negative core evaluation about people and oneself. Fortunately for this boy, the mother recognized that something was wrong and took action to identify and correct her son's mistaken conclusion.[5]

The way in which this mother handled her son's fear of school is a model of what parents and teachers should be doing on a regular basis. The mother's questioning, it must be emphasized, was performed in a loving and supportive manner. She did not sermonize or criticize

---

[4]Packer, "Understanding the Subconscious," 11–12.

[5]"It is not the child's experiences which dictate his actions; it is the conclusions which he draws from his experiences. . . . We cannot say, for example, that if a child is badly nourished he will become a criminal. We must see what conclusion the child has drawn [from this experience]" (brackets supplied by the Ansbachers). Alfred Adler, quoted in Heinz L. Ansbacher and Rowena R. Ansbacher, eds., *The Individual Psychology of Alfred Adler: A Systematic Presentation in Selections from His Writings* (New York: Harper Torchbook, 1964), 209. Adler clearly anticipated cognitive psychology. Albert Ellis and Aaron Beck are said to be leading founders of the theory. Ellis compared his "rational-emotive-behavior therapy" to Adler's psychology in this article: Albert Ellis, "Rational Psychotherapy and Individual Psychology," *Journal of Individual Psychology* 13, no. 1 (1957), 38–44.

or cross-examine like a merciless defense attorney. Had the mother done so, or ignored her son's emotions altogether and forced him to go to school, his negative conclusions about other people and himself could have solidified quickly and he could even have soon begun to form defense values or other defensive habits.

Both defense values and the other defensive habits are automatized, subconscious attempts to protect us against self-doubt and anxiety. Much mention throughout this work has been made of both, so it is time to discuss their operation. They both begin consciously and that would be the ideal time to catch them in a young person, to teach the skill of introspection to prevent further occurrences and to make corrections of what does occur.

THE DEFENSIVE HABITS AND HOW THEY OPERATE

Self-doubt is the opposite of self-esteem and is what it sounds like: doubt about, or distrust of, oneself, but it is a doubt or distrust that applies to our whole selves as being unfit to live, or to a part of ourselves. Its emotional expression is pathological anxiety, which is not the same as an objectively valid fear. Pathological anxiety is a seemingly causeless fear, one that has no objectively or rationally valid object.[6] In Packer's words, the doubt in the evaluation of our whole selves says, "There is a danger that my whole being is 'wrong' in some way. I cannot cope with life."[7] Symptoms include panic, a sense of impending doom, excessive or prolonged fear, inability to act, and a variety of psychosomatic ailments.

Pathological anxiety is not healthy because there is no demonstrable threat. We *feel* unworthy or unable, but there is nothing that presents us with a genuine danger. In contrast, a bear on the path in a woods where we are walking would likely cause objective, rationally valid fear in all but the most experienced bear specialist. The anxiety of self-doubt is experienced as life-threatening, especially by children,

---

[6] The object and cause of pathological anxiety is the self-doubt, but sufferers usually do not recognize it.

[7] Packer, "Art of Introspection," 229.

but as Packer states, "the life that is being threatened is the *psychological life* of the person." In extreme cases it is the feeling of being fundamentally no good.[8]

Habits of Defense

In chapter 3, I used the example of a father yelling at his child and calling him names for spilling the milk.[9] Objectively, spilling the milk is not a misdeed justifying the father's behavior, though the dad's behavior is a good example of why adults need to be educated in psychology and learn better ways of relating to their kids. Children in such situations often do not know how to respond, so they may experience self-doubt and anxiety accompanied by an urgency to minimize or eliminate the feeling. In the absence of guidance from adults, this is where suppression, a conscious process, begins.

The most important defensive habit is repression, because it is the foundation and support of all others, and in contrast to what Freud says, is never healthy. Children begin by consciously suppressing, that is, by willfully putting painful feelings out of their minds. They tell themselves, "I don't want to feel this way." Repeated enough times in similar situations, a habit becomes established with the standing order not to be aware of negative feelings, especially "when people yell at me and call me names." The repressing becomes automatized and subconscious, which means the child no longer has to think about it in order not to

---

[8] Packer, "Art of Introspection," 228 (italics added). Because we are not omniscient, nor is the use of reason automatic, everyone at one time or another can experience a narrower form of localized self-doubt, pertaining, say, to one particular action. Packer relates a hypothetical story of herself at a gym. An instructor—Miss Perfect Shape, Packer calls her—solicitously offers Packer advice. Packer's reaction? "I can assure you that Miss Perfect Shape could cause me some self-doubt." Packer, "Art of Introspection," 233. There also is such a thing as objective or normal anxiety that perhaps should be called worry or nervousness, such as the concern we might feel when starting a new job or having to stand up in front of an audience (stage fright). The feeling stems from not knowing exactly what is going to happen and whether or not we can handle the situation. A certain edge or uneasiness may be felt, though depending on our psychologies, there also may be an additional dose of pathological anxiety operating. Branden, *Psychology of Self-Esteem*, 153–60. Packer, "Art of Introspection," 231.

[9] See above, p. 92.

feel the pain. The repression may even generalize to, and be triggered by, any raised voice that is within earshot but not directed at the child. Defensive habits are involuntary subconscious responses to events that activate self-doubt; their aim is to distract or divert attention from the anxiety. In the case of repression, a standing order controls our perception and says, "Don't be aware of the unpleasantness that is being triggered"; its aim is to block or bar the feeling.[10]

Emotions per se, however, are not repressed. It is the evaluation— I'm bad because I spilled the milk—that gives rise to the negative, painful emotion in the child and is therefore the target of repression. Included in the evaluation are the emotion's meaning, intensity, and object, which also can be repressed.[11] Repression is an "automatized avoidance reaction," as Nathaniel Branden puts it, "always directed at thoughts." The thoughts may be positive or negative, good or bad. Freud concentrated on the repression of negatives. Branden points out that we can also repress what is positive—good and healthy in us—due, say, to faulty ideas we have been taught, such as religion that tells us it is selfish to be independent and idealistic.[12] In some of the worst family upbringings, children may be taught that feeling anger or even any emotion is bad.[13]

---

[10]Packer, "Anger," in *Lectures on Psychology*, 111. Packer, "Toward a Lasting Romantic Relationship, Part II," in *Lectures on Psychology*, 188–90. The creative process, to emphasize the difference between creative thinking and repression, says "Be aware." Repression says, "Don't be aware."

[11]But, once again, trauma cannot be repressed, whether it be the memory of Holocaust torture, the witnessing of violent crime or gunfire, or the memory of having been wounded in an assault or abused physically or sexually. Allowing for the fading of some detail over time, the memories of such victims are vivid and highly accurate. McHugh, *Try to Remember*, 46. To call it in these cases "repressed memory" or "repressed trauma" is false.

[12]Branden, *Psychology of Self-Esteem*, 77, 87, and chap. 5 throughout. Branden, *Vision of Ayn Rand*, 53–54 and chap. 20.

[13]Quoting Packer, "I want to emphasize that the subconscious cannot make choices. As a result, repression spreads like cancer. In this way, all emotions, including positive ones, get repressed. And in extreme cases, the individual becomes totally deadened emotionally." Packer, "Romantic Relationship, Part II," 189. "Deadened emotionally," to beat this issue a bit more, is the worst that results from repression, *not* amnesia of sexual trauma. It is not the memory of a specific event that is repressed. It is the unwanted, repressed cluster of emotions involved in the

Repression does not work. It is an attempt to drive pain away, but it cannot completely do so. Packer gives examples of how repressed evaluations, and therefore the emotions caused by them, may rise to consciousness. One person might say, "I'm not angry, I'm never angry," though his teeth are clenched tight. And another might say, "I'm not afraid—maybe I'm slightly uncomfortable, but definitely not afraid."[14] Still another person in the present might complain about a discomfort toward her mother, and perhaps even say that she does not like her. Upon examination, this person may discover repressed evaluations from childhood that her mother was controlling and undercutting, which over time generalized, or rather, overgeneralized, into a conclusion that her mother was evil. The solution through introspection in therapy was to reevaluate the earlier evaluations to correct the past overgeneralization.

Because repression does not work, the boy in the example of being yelled at over spilled milk may resort to "helper" defenses, such as denial, responding to his father and others who accuse him of accidents by saying that he was not the culprit. He may also deny that he feels any pain at all when yelled at. Or he may adopt the defensive habit of projection, attributing the cause to others, say, the boy's sister. Because both repression and the helper defenses begin on the conscious level, an observant parent may be able to catch them in the making and prevent them from becoming firmly established habits.

Although some people become dominated by certain defensive habits and we might say that they are, for example, a "hostile personality" or a "withdrawn personality," the habits themselves are activated by a specific event that prompts the self-doubt. In order to catch defensive habits in the making, knowledgeable and loving adults must not themselves have bad psychological habits and, at the same time, must understand how to introspect and teach introspection.

---

event that may accompany some normal fading of the memory. Repression is not amnesia, nor is it forgetting. It is an attempt to mute emotions. The triggering event and its memory are still there on some level.

[14] Packer, "Romantic Relationship, Part II," 189–90.

Values of Defense

Defense values operate in a similar manner, as they are a special case of defensive habit, but they require separate discussion. If the boy in the example of the spilled milk had energetically cleaned up the mess and the father gushingly praised him as "a good little boy" for making amends to his mistake, the boy may have begun to develop a defense value. Profuse praise can lead to such beginnings.[15]

Defense values are self-esteem substitutes, a pseudo-self-esteem, that give us a false sense of specialness in relation to others or a superiority over them. The purpose of a defense value is to deflect attention from our feelings of unworthiness and inefficacy. Defense values may be any value, rational or irrational. The way the values are held in our minds and pursued are what makes them defensive. Feeling a jolt of excitement when thinking or talking about the value and especially bragging to others are signs that a defense value is operating.[16] For example, the rational value of making delicious creamed spinach can become defensive when the cook boasts, "I make the best creamed spinach ever. I know you'll love it!" And on the irrational side of values, the thief brags, "I shoplift and never get caught!"

Defense values are pretensions to self-esteem, and are other-directed. They are not pursued for themselves as genuine values. Once formed, defense values, like the other defensive habits, become automatized and can be activated by specific events, such as a cocktail party conversation that brings up cooking. Or they may be held as a persistent feeling of oneself, say as an artist or person of artistic sensibility. The cook may or may not be a good cook of creamed spinach and the artist may be a good artist, or may not paint at all. The bragging and pretensions are the

---

[15] Branden, *Psychology of Self-Esteem*, 146. Packer, "Romantic Relationship, Part II," 185–87. The term "defense value" was coined by Branden, but the concept goes back at least to Karen Horney in her notion of the search for glory through self-idealization. Karen Horney, *Neurosis and Human Growth: The Struggle toward Self-Realization* (New York: W. W. Norton, 1950), 17–39. "Defense value" is not unrelated to Freud's term "narcissism" (and the myth of Narcissus).

[16] Also, "getting mileage," as Packer puts it, is another sign that a defense value may be operating, that is, "reliving over and over again some incident in which a trait or skill . . . gained positive recognition." Packer, "Interview with Edith Packer," 298.

defenses against anxiety. Sometimes a split occurs, along with denial, between the "real me" and "the acting me." The "real me" is the artist of refined sensibility; the "acting me" is the one who does not paint.[17]

It is often the adults' praise of young children that encourages the development of defense values, such as, "You're a good little boy for being daddy's helper."[18] But as Haim Ginott says, "Direct praise of personality, like direct sunlight, is uncomfortable and blinding," and "It creates anxiety, invites dependency, and evokes defensiveness."[19] Praise, nonetheless, feels good to children, especially those who are neglected by their parents or are routinely berated. The parental praise becomes a sign to children that they are worthy and competent, at least in their parents' eyes. Self-esteem, however, does not derive from such judgments of us made by others, but the children do not know it. Thus, they actively and often unwisely—by adopting the helper defense of compulsion—seek more of the same kind of praise. The defense value becomes firmly established and pursued as a habitual behavior.[20]

To catch defense values in the making, it is important, first, that adults refrain from glowing praise and adopt Ginott's previously mentioned principle to describe without evaluating.[21] Second, observation

---

[17] The third chapter of Horney's book is titled "The Tyranny of the Should," a reference to all the "shoulds" we think we ought to do "somehow" or ought to be "somehow." This last—I believe I first heard it from Allan Blumenthal—has been called "somehow thinking." When we have no plans or specific steps to take toward achieving our values, we may still think, for example, we *should* be that great artist "somehow." Horney, *Neurosis and Human Growth*, chap. 3.

[18] In her practice Packer observed that defense values usually develop first in children, followed later by the other defensive habits.

[19] The first quotation is from Ginott, *Between Parent & Child*, 47, and the second from Ginott, *Teacher & Child: A Book for Parents and Teachers* (New York: Collier Books, 1972), 125.

[20] The list of potential defense values is endless. "I'm good at sports, cooking, cleaning, schoolwork. I'm intelligent, I have a lot of friends, I have talent, I have great potential," and so on. Defense values are formed with reference to a group of people, initially usually our parents and relatives, but they expand outward to friends, teachers, coworkers, and any other group we consider "significant others." Defense values set ourselves up as superior to the group's outsiders and special in the eyes of the insiders. They are key in the formation of dependent personalities.

[21] See above, p. 92. Stated simply, Ginott's principle, whether involving praise or criticism, is: "Describe, don't evaluate. Let the child draw the evaluative conclusion."

of and discussion with the child are necessary to discern how values are being held, with bragging, again, being a good indicator of the presence of a defense value.

Detecting and correcting defense values or other defensive habits or core evaluations is not an easy task. This takes us to the more general discussion of introspection—for ourselves and as instruction on how to help our children and students learn to introspect.

INTROSPECTING EMOTIONS AND CORE EVALUATIONS

Introspection, according to Packer, applies both broadly and narrowly to all areas of our inner selves:

> The process of introspection . . . can include an examination of the conscious mind's efficiency in thinking, the discovery of subconscious connections in making evaluations, the discovery of intermediate or core evaluations, the identification of defense mechanisms, and the discovery and identification of one's values of every kind, from fundamental to trivial.[22]

Parents and teachers in particular need to help children and students identify their own emotions and core evaluations, and to correct the mistaken ones. Let us begin by considering the process of introspecting emotions; core evaluations follow as part of that process.

Like the defensive habits, emotions are activated or triggered by a perceived object, person, or event, or even in our imagination by the thought of an object, person, or event. Unlike the defenses, emotions per se cannot properly be described as habitual behaviors, as they are lightning-quick psychosomatic responses to previously formed evaluations being applied to a new object. In a narrower sense, though, emotional responses are learned and like unwanted habitual behaviors can be changed. The learned component of emotion is our evaluations.[23]

---

[22] Packer, "Art of Introspection," 223.

[23] Aristotle was probably the first to identify that evaluations stand behind emotions and that rational and irrational desires derive, respectively, from correct and incorrect evaluations. See Alexander Nehamas, "Pity and Fear in the *Rhetoric* and the *Poetics*," in Amélie Rorty, ed., *Essays on Aristotle's Poetics* (Princteon, NJ: Princeton University Press, 1992), 297.

To illustrate the importance of evaluations in understanding emotions, consider the following. Puppies and young children in their early lives do not know they should avoid the path of an oncoming car. Running into the street will not automatically cause them to feel fear, unless the sounds of screeching brakes and screams of pet owner or parent are heard. Even then they still may not know to get out of the street. The process of evaluating, like the process of identifying facts, is a part of learning; it requires us to declare something as either beneficial or harmful. This is what a value judgment is.[24] When we see, that is, perceive, something that we value or disvalue, we will automatically experience the response called an emotion, with both physiological and psychological components.[25]

And it is those value judgments that can be right or wrong, true or false. When a toddler picks up what to the toddler is a beautiful, multi-colored squiggly thing, mom screams in horror, because the squiggly thing is a deadly coral snake. Adults, of course, also make mistakes, say, when we hear a loud noise, judge it to be a gunshot and, consequently, feel fear. In fact, it was only the backfire of an automobile. When we identify the source of the noise, our emotion of fear withers away.

The capacity to experience emotions is inborn, but the specific emotion we will feel depends on our correct or incorrect perception of the object, person, or event and our correct or incorrect stored, subconscious value judgment of the object, person, or event as beneficial or harmful to us.[26] The source and cause of emotions is not mysterious, but their identification takes work. Can we catch emotions in the

---

[24]Value judgments are often contrasted to judgments of fact, but the distinction between facts and values is superficial. Saying that "Socrates is mortal" and that he is "evil, threatening, or dangerous" are both judgments of facts. Value judgments, because they can also be either true or false, are a special case of fact judgments.

[25]When we experience an emotion, our breathing, blood pressure, and perspiration can be affected. We can also feel a tendency or desire to act. In this discussion, I am focusing only on the psychological aspects of emotion.

[26]There are two steps in the formation of an emotion. First, the fact judgment— that is a coral snake. Second, the value judgment—that coral snake can kill me. Either can be true or false.

making, before they become automatized? Yes, but we must understand the process of introspecting emotions in ourselves to know how to catch them in the making—in us, as well as in our children and students. To this process, we now turn.

The Identifying Steps

Introspecting emotions requires us first to name the emotion, then identify its universal and personal evaluations. For some adults, naming an emotion can be challenging, and young children have not yet learned how to put words or concepts to much of their experience, especially their psychological experience. Adults, for example, may say they are "upset," but "upset" is not a single emotion. It is a cluster, often of anger, disappointment, and hurt. And children may not be able to respond when an adult asks, "What are you feeling?" Or, they may immediately say "yes" to whatever emotion the adult suggests, not understanding what the question means. Introspection begins by naming the emotion, and those seeking to educate children and students for independence must learn to teach their charges how to identify what they are feeling.[27]

Recognizing that a universal abstract evaluation underlies each emotion should assist the identification of the emotion being experienced. The perceived gunshot described above evokes fear in us because of our judgment that the sound means danger or that something is threatening us. The judgment of danger, or conclusion of the presence of a threat, is the universal abstract evaluation underlying fear. To give a few more examples, the evaluation behind anger says, "an injustice has been done to me"; the thought behind joy says, "I have achieved one of my most important values"; and the conclusion behind disappointment would be, "I didn't get what I wanted."[28]

---

[27] What follows is a discussion aimed at adults so they may learn what needs to be taught to children and students. Adolescents should also be able to follow and benefit. It is based on Packer, "Art of Introspection," with portions on identifying core evaluations based on "Understanding the Subconscious."

[28] Packer, "Anger," 111–12 and "Art of Introspection," 226–35.

Each emotion, assuming we are not talking about a cluster like "upset," expresses a unique evaluation that is universal, which means it is present in all instances of the emotion, and the universal is abstract because it does not incorporate the concrete circumstances in which the emotion arises. To further determine the full meaning of an emotion to us, we must recognize and identify what Packer calls our personal evaluation, the active, inner conversation we have about the concretes of the situation that triggered the emotion. Seeing a bear on our path in the woods would likely trigger fear in most of us. The inner conversation we have at that moment might be: "I'm going to die. I have to get out of here!" Or, the thoughts of a child whose lunch money has been stolen might be: "That *#%@ [not-so-nice modifier] Johnny is a thief and a bum. I want my money back!" A child who cries when something like this occurs would also be feeling hurt and might be saying, "I liked Johnny but now I can't trust him."[29]

It is these inner conversations, or personal language or voice, as Packer also describes them, that constitute the unique way in which we experience and hold in our minds the concretes of the emotion-causing situation. The inner conversation is our personal evaluation that when abstracted from the concretes becomes universal. Thus, people who feel angry will have as many different inner conversations and personal evaluations as there are different concretes that give rise to the emotion, but their universal evaluations underlying the anger will be the same, namely that an injustice has been done to them. The significance of uncovering personal evaluations is that although we may be able to identify what we are feeling and perhaps even the universal

---

[29] Our inner lives are quite active, with perhaps hundreds or even thousands of thoughts per day. All of Packer's lectures provide an abundance of extended case examples of non-criminal inner conversations. For the criminal mind, see Stanton Samenow. I continue to refer to Samenow, because his work has identified the unexpected—to most of us, I believe—number of inner conversations that criminals have with themselves to justify their crimes. Samenow especially illuminates what works up criminals to commit the so-called crime of passion, which is neither sudden nor passionate, but the end result of many months or years of festering inner hatred. Something similar can be said about why we non-criminals feel and do what we feel and do, in the sense that it all begins in our inner conversations, from an early age.

evaluation of the emotion, we may not know why we are feeling that emotion. Discovering the personal evaluation and its inner conversation at the time of the emotion's occurrence gives us that underlying cause.

As Packer points out, the discovery of personal evaluations may help us uncover emotions we were previously unaware of, especially if we tend to be repressed. Depending on the severity of our repression, we may feel only a muted emotion or in extreme cases not much at all, except perhaps a vague uneasiness or fear of emotions in general. To help us uncover our personal evaluations, Packer suggests that we "go over carefully the concretes of the previous day" and ask ourselves, "What do I really think about this fact? What do I think an unrepressed person would feel under the circumstances?" And "write down all the details in the form of a monologue."[30]

Performing this task of introspection, says Packer, may surprise us as to how much inner conversation goes on in our minds every day, especially in relation to specific concrete events. The task is not easy and we may tend to rush through and minimize our discoveries, or condemn ourselves for the negative emotions we find. Such a result, says Packer, sabotages the subsequent, even more important steps of the process. We must resist rushing or minimizing, and, especially, condemning ourselves.[31]

Assessing the Evaluations

The introspective, identifying steps can give us insight into what goes on in our minds, but insight alone is not enough to correct inappropriate, painful, or out-of-context emotions, nor is it the end or goal of introspective competence. We must evaluate the evaluations and, if incorrect, identify why they are incorrect,

---

[30]Packer, "Art of Introspection," 237–38.

[31]It is important to emphasize that "we feel what we feel," which means there is nothing wrong, bad, or immoral about experiencing any emotion (or fantasy, for that matter). Contrary to what most religions say, including in particular Christianity, it is not a sin to feel an emotion. Out-of-context or any other emotions (or fantasies) that we may feel say nothing about our character. Action determines who we are as a moral person.

then act to correct them. Once the evaluations are changed, the emotions will follow.[32]

Emotions are automatic responses to evaluations, so emotions per se cannot be incorrect, but the evaluation can be false and lead us to express, say, anger unjustly. This would occur if the person we are angry at for supposedly doing us an injustice in fact did not do so. Checking the facts on which our evaluations rest becomes crucial. If Johnny did not take my lunch money—I discovered that it fell out of my pocket on the playground—I no longer have cause to be angry at him, or to feel hurt. Often, however, our inappropriate emotions are not this simple. A young woman attracted to men who are abusive is not in any sense accurately seeing the men as potential romantic soulmates. Her false evaluation about love and the men she is attracted to is likely caused by deeper, subconscious issues, especially core evaluations and her mid-level evaluations about the opposite sex, which means her sexual self-confidence.[33]

Indeed, the facts that are evaluated at this step may be filtered and misinterpreted by mistaken core evaluations (to be discussed further below) or by defensive habits that block their clear perception. Compartmentalization, for example, can lead us to interpret facts differently, or selectively, depending on which "compartment" of our mind, and its method of thinking, is operating. In the split between professional and personal life that I have mentioned several times before, it is not uncommon for some of us to be scrupulously objective when perceiving facts at work, but abandon all responsibility when judging friends

---

[32]If the evaluations are correct, the process would stop with this step.

[33]Thinking errors (most likely subconscious emotional generalizations) in the development of our masculinity and femininity are also what lead to same-sex attraction, which I hasten to add is neither immoral nor in any sense a "sin." For a lengthy discussion of sexual self-confidence, though not explicitly analyzing same-sex attractions, see Packer, "Romantic Relationship, Part II," 168–78. Masculinity and femininity are emotional styles expressed as an attitude toward ourselves as a male or female person in relation to the opposite sex. Both derive from our different anatomies and physiologies and are not arbitrary. Cf. Branden, *Psychology of Self-Esteem*, chap. 11. See New Zealanders N. E. and B. K. Whitehead for the case that same-sex attraction is not genetically determined, *My Genes Made Me Do It*. The Whiteheads have reviewed over 10,000 studies and publications.

or spouses. The split, of course, can also go in the other direction; we can be scrupulously objective and honest in personal relationships, but not so at work. It is the irrational side of the split that leads to unhappiness, generating inappropriate, painful and out-of-context emotions, as well as inappropriate and harmful conduct.

To aid investigating our evaluations, says Packer, we can ask ourselves several questions. "Do I have *all* the facts?" One new detail can change a conclusion, as it did in the lunch money example. "Am I resisting or ignoring certain facts?" Resistance, due to subconscious factors, can hamper our objectivity in this step. It means knowledge of our psychologies and our specific methods of thinking now become relevant. "Do we have tendencies to deny, dismiss, exaggerate, or overgeneralize?" Facts become tainted under such mental policies and we must exert extra effort to counter the tendencies. Will identifying an evaluation as incorrect automatically change our emotions? No, because there is nothing automatic about changing psychologies that have built up and been reinforced through habitual behavior over many months or years. Underlying those habits are our core evaluations, with defense values and the other defensive habits also playing a role, but let us concentrate on discovering core evaluations.

Discovering the Reasons for Mistaken Evaluations

We now must examine the reasons why we hold those incorrect evaluations in the first place, which means uncovering the mistaken core evaluations that influence our present value judgments. For the more we know about and understand our core evaluations, the more easily we will be able to discover why we have made mistaken evaluations, and the more easily we will be able to teach a similar process, albeit on a more elementary level, to our children and students.[34]

Consider two cases of mistaken evaluations. One, an out-of-context emotion of extreme anger or even hostility at someone who has just stepped in front of us in a movie line. The second, an extreme fear

---

[34] This step is the most difficult and some adults and children may require professional help.

of talking to anyone in a social gathering. Why the anger and hostility over a minor slight that may even have been inadvertent? And why the almost paralytic inability to initiate or sustain a conversation in a situation in which all of the people are clearly kind? The two cases involve emotions that are overreactions to the facts, that is, misperceptions such that the evaluations behind the emotions are wrong. Neither situation is harmful or threatening. What is the cause of these reactions?

The overreactions are defenses against self-doubt and anxiety and such overreactions are often generated by a core evaluation, supported by defensive habits. In the first case, the core evaluation might be something like, "People always take advantage of me," supported by hostility. In the second case, it might be, "People are dangerous. I must be careful around them," supported by paranoia and, perhaps, withdrawal. These evaluations are universal like the ones underlying specific emotions, but they apply globally to each person's personality. Thus, when an event in the present is similar to the original events in one's earlier life that led to the formation of a core evaluation, the subconscious core evaluation takes over to perceive and interpret the present in light of those past events.

In addition, unidentified, mistaken core evaluations may lead us, almost as if we are drawn by a "negative magnet," to seek instances in which we will feel taken advantage of or rejected and humiliated. In other words, we may seek instances in which we see people as mean and threatening, never noticing the friendly ones, or we may seek instances in which we confirm our unworthiness and incompetence and conclude that the world is going to hell. Discovering core evaluations and correcting the mistaken ones is essential to living a happy life and to teaching the same to our children and students.

Packer provides several tips on how to discover core evaluations.[35] Dreams, though she hastens to add that she is not a Freudian, may give clues for further exploration, such as a "symbolic representation of especially painful experiences from childhood." Defensive habits

---

[35] Packer "Understanding the Subconscious," 19–24.

themselves, because they are manifested as an overt behavior, can also provide clues, as a starting point. Emotions—out-of-context or in general, as an overall attitude or sense of life—provide universal and personal evaluations that have been influenced by, or have generated, our core evaluations; as a result, they also provide good starting points for discovery.[36] Early recollections from before age seven or eight, discussed or written down in the present tense, says Packer, provide especially strong clues to the origin and formation of core evaluations.[37] Finally, trauma or a dominating injury from childhood can yield information, although coping with and healing such injuries may require the aid of a professional therapist.

Similar patterns of discovery can be followed to uncover mid-level evaluations and the processes and triggers of defensive habits. Discovering core and mid-level evaluations, however, and the operation of our defensive habits, along with a cathartic re-experiencing of the originating events of the mistakes, is not sufficient to change our thinking and thereby automatically make us happy. Corrective action is the most important and last step in introspecting our emotions.

Corrective Action to Change Habits

Driving a car is an acquired habit with knowledge and skill that has been programmed in our subconscious. We do not have to think much about driving. We just do it through mental and muscle memory. Standing orders encourage us to watch out for other drivers and highway hazards. We drive as if on "autopilot" but our conscious mind can take over at any moment. We can acquire bad driving habits, such as changing lanes without looking or signaling or slamming the brakes at every intersection. Such habits can be changed but they require extra effort.

---

[36] Packer's favored technique here is to ask the patient, "What would the emotion say if it could talk?"

[37] Packer borrows this technique from Alfred Adler, adding that the recollections be discussed or written in present tense. Packer, "Understanding the Subconscious," 21–22.

Our psychologies are similar. We live by mental habits, guided by our subconsciously stored core and mid-level evaluations that in effect put us on "autopilot" and give us standing orders. Some mental habits are good, some are bad. At any time, we can exert conscious control over our overt behavior to ensure that we do not do anything harmful, illegal, or immoral, such as take drugs, steal money, or cheat on our spouses or business partners. Such conscious control is called "will power," even though urges to do otherwise may still be present. Those "urges" derive from our core and mid-level evaluations, plus the other evaluations underlying our emotions. All urges—the mental habits by which we live—have been acquired and programmed by us. They can be changed.[38]

Core evaluations, says Packer, are built up brick by brick in childhood, so they also must be taken apart brick by brick and rebuilt. The same applies to our mid-level evaluations and all others underlying our emotions. The task is easier for specific emotions than for the more fundamental evaluations that have been automatized from an early age. This again is why we would like to catch in the making these developing core and mid-level evaluations—in ourselves and in our children and students.

Changing a habit requires practice. It requires awareness of the instances in which the bad habit operates. It requires conscious monitoring of our thoughts and behavior leading up to and during the instance.[39] And it requires us willfully to use different, that is, good, thoughts and behaviors to counter the bad ones. Repetition in similar instances automatizes the skill, thus reprogramming our

---

[38]This is not to make light of how strong the urges may be in some of us, especially entrenched habits of alcohol or drug addiction. Also, the older we get the stronger our mental habits become and the more difficult it is to resist them and change. Many people give up and settle for a less happy life. The conscious will power, however, is still there and it can be applied if one chooses to do so.

[39]I have used the word "monitor" throughout this work as a concept closely related to introspection. I learned it from Allan Blumenthal. See his book *Identity, Inner Life and Psychological Change*, 91–92, 108–110. Dr. Blumenthal would emphasize that when we monitor our mental processes, we need to slow them down like a film strip to examine our thoughts frame by frame.

subconscious in relation to the specific habit. Corrective action is the ultimate aim of introspective competence.

Consider our example of the young man who is petrified to ask girls out on dates. Through the earlier steps of introspection he has discovered that his expectation of danger is based on his personal evaluation that girls can see what an unworthy bum he is, they also supposedly have x-ray vision into his subconscious, and they may even bite his head off, figuratively, though he feels it literally. Further introspection reveals his defensive habit of withdrawal from most anything social, especially involving girls, and that this defense developed from his core evaluation that people are dangerous, which may have developed from his reactions to the way his mother treated him, as well as his mid-level evaluation that he is not "man enough" to ask an attractive girl for a date.

This young man now realizes that he has automatized mental habits that have retarded the development of his social and romantic skills. To change these habits, he must reprogram his subconscious by developing and repeating to himself new thoughts and personal language, namely that girls are not his mother, that he is not an unworthy or ugly bum, and that the girls might even be nice to him. Next, though, is the hardest part. He must put himself in situations where he might be able to ask a girl for date, that is, go to parties and other social gatherings. He must be aware of his fear, remind himself of his rehearsed new thoughts, then act by asking a real girl.[40] He may be surprised to discover that some girls will say, "Thank you. I'd love to." And others may say, "I have a boyfriend . . . but thank you," followed by a big smile. Repeated practice in these situations and awareness that his head was not bitten off should gradually change the young man's mental habits about dating.

Other issues in our psychologies may be more complicated and require more time to sort out. The significance of this discussion on introspection and the essential point to teach our children and students is that we control our lives. Our behavior is determined by what we have

---

[40]Rehearsal in front of a mirror or with a friend can help. Keeping a journal to record one's false personal evaluations, as well as the new ones, can also help. Action is still required.

put in our minds and we can change that content. Paraphrasing William Glasser, "We choose our own misery, so also we can choose our own happiness." Genes and environment may influence us, but they do not control us.[41]

Two final quotations from Packer emphasize the importance for all of us to introspect our emotions and core evaluations, and to teach the skill to the young. On emotions, Packer says:

> Understanding your emotions enables you to get in touch with what is uniquely you: your individuality. The more you know what you value, the greater is your sense of your own identity and the more you will know who you are.[42]

And by extension, we might add, the greater our sense of identity and the stronger it becomes, the greater our development toward independence and a strong desire to maintain and express independent judgment.

On core evaluations, Packer says this:

> Parents cannot guarantee that children will evaluate their experiences correctly, but by knowing about the existence of core evaluations, they may be able to help prevent the formation of seriously distorted ones, capable of hampering or crippling a child throughout his life. . . . I have never been more hopeful . . . than I am now about the ability of psychology to help people overcome their problems. The real hope, however, is in the future, in a far improved understanding of the connections between childhood injury and core evaluations.[43]

TEACHING INTROSPECTION

Innovators in history have often exhibited independent judgment in the face of opposition, but few probably stopped to examine their inner thoughts, other than what project they were focusing on in their

---

[41]Glasser, *Choice Theory*, 1.

[42]Packer, "Art of Introspection," 221.

[43]Packer, "Understanding the Subconscious," 25–26. In *Montessori, Dewey, and Capitalism*, 142n50, I coined the acronym NUPARC to help learn the art of introspection. The steps are as follows: **N**ame the emotion, then the **U**niversal and **P**ersonal evaluations. **A**ssess the evaluations against the facts, identify the **R**easons for the incorrect evaluations, then **C**orrect and reinforce new premises through practice. Packer's art of introspection using this acronym has been taught with success in college critical thinking courses.

professional lives. (Freud would be an exception; Socrates also, to some extent.) And these innovators also presumably did not possess the mental inhibitions that prevent or restrain others from pursuing their goals, or even choosing sound goals. We know little about the innovators' psychologies in either their professional or personal lives. They almost seem to have been born mentally healthy.

For most of the rest of us, the skill of introspection is necessary to maintain and improve our self-esteem. The skill is also necessary, though not sufficient, to support and advance the free society, by developing in many of its citizens the psychology of independence and independent judgment. Introspective competence is especially necessary to teach to children and students before any of their unhealthy mental habits become ingrained. The question is, how should we go about teaching introspection?

As in teaching anything, the teacher's thorough understanding of the subject matter comes first, and that has been summarized above, though much more can be found in Edith Packer's book *Lectures on Psychology*. Prerequisite to such teaching, certain premises must be understood as self-evident and employed with meticulous sincerity, such as: no coercion or other attempts to control the child or student, which means no corporal punishment or hitting of any kind and no yelling or screaming, especially in the form of name calling, criticizing, blaming, nagging, or threatening.[44] This means accepting the child's emotions, not denying them with such injurious statements as, "You don't really feel that" or "You don't mean that" or, worse, "Go in the other room until you feel better—and stop crying!" These are all prescriptions for repression and, depending on the child, rebellion or submissiveness and dependence.

---

[44]In other words, Glasser's deadly habits that destroy relationships: criticizing, blaming, complaining, nagging, threatening, punishing, and bribing (rewarding to control). Glasser, *Unhappy Teenagers*, 13. In addition, negative comments to children about ourselves, other people, and the world should also be omitted from these relationships. Children inhale what valued adults, especially parents, say and do, often adopting their significant others' core and mid-level evaluations. Errors we have made in our earlier lives can and should be acknowledged and discussed.

The fundamental relationship of adult to child is one of nurture, to feed and clothe the child for physical health and well-being, and, more significantly, to feed and clothe the child's mind with the knowledge and skill required to develop and maintain mental health and well-being. Psychological nurture means teaching introspective competence, and introspective competence is the essential requirement for both flourishing of the individual and advancement of civilization.[45]

Once the subject matter of introspection is understood, the next challenge is to communicate it and to encourage, train, and supervise development of the skill. The talents required of parent and teacher are those of a coach. The first task of a good coach is to adapt the subject matter of a skill to age, stage of development, and context of knowledge of the child. A five-year-old must be taught in a different way than a ten- or fifteen-year-old.[46]

Regrettably, introspection for over a hundred years has been viewed as unscientific, pseudo-scientific, and even non-existent by psychologists and psychotherapists. Models of teaching introspection, especially to young children, are themselves therefore nearly non-existent. What follows is at best a sketch or outline of how to teach the skill.

Most important for young children is awareness of what they are feeling, the knowledge and approval that it is okay for them to feel whatever they might be feeling, and the knowledge and approval that it is good to talk about feelings with their—non-judgmental—parents and teachers. "Most children," as Packer says, "do not share many of their important thoughts and emotions with their parents," but getting

---

[45] A minimal library for parents and teachers should include the following works: Haim Ginott, *Between Parent & Child* and *Teacher & Child*; Thomas Gordon, *Parent Effectiveness Training* and *Teacher Effectiveness Training*; Alfie Kohn, *Unconditional Parenting*; William Glasser, *The Quality School*. See also Nathaniel Branden, *Six Pillars of Self-Esteem* (New York: Bantam, 1994), chap. 13 and 14, which discuss the nurturing of self-esteem by both parents and teachers. The library should include all works from the literature of nurture, *not* the literature of obedience to authority.

[46] "Good coach," it must be emphasized, is one who is decidedly *not* authoritarian. Some youth coaches seem to think that anger and coercion are the essence of coaching.

young children to do so is probably the single most important accomplishment a parent or teacher can realize in teaching introspection.[47] Adults must become keen observers of their children's words and behavior. Emotions, such as anger or fear, can be readily discerned, but silence or reticence to talk can mean many different things. It can mean embarrassment, shame, hurt, or similar negative emotions, or nothing in particular. Exploratory discussions can draw children out.

When children talk, they often do so in code and adults must become expert at decrypting the message. Haim Ginott's book *Between Parent & Child* begins with a little boy asking his father how many abandoned children there are in Harlem. The father proceeded to give a detailed lecture on the subject, but the boy followed up with additional questions, "What about New York City? What about the United States? What about Europe?" Finally, the father realized that his son was asking about himself, "Will I be abandoned?" The conversation immediately changed to the father's love and reassurance that nothing of the kind will ever happen.[48]

Another little boy, on his first day at kindergarten blurted out, "Who painted these ugly pictures? Who broke this toy?" His mother was embarrassed, but the teacher knew the code. She responded by saying, "Toys are for playing. Sometimes they get broken. It happens." The boy was asking what happens to kids who break toys (and paint ugly pictures). Answer: nothing, but the boy needed to hear this from an adult to both acknowledge his anxiety and eliminate it.[49]

A twelve-year-old girl's cousin went home after a summer stay. The girl cried and complained, "I'll be all alone." Her mother, unfortunately, was dismissive and called her daughter names: "You'll get over it. You're such a crybaby." Ginott recommends that the mother should have said the following: "It will be lonely without Susie, it is hard to be apart," and "the house must seem kind of empty." About these recommendations, Ginott says, "Such responses create intimacy between parent and child,"

---

[47] Packer, "Understanding the Subconscious," 12.

[48] Ginott, *Between Parent & Child*, 21–22.

[49] Ginott, *Between Parent & Child*, 22.

instead of distance. The daughter will now feel understood because her loneliness and hurt have been acknowledged. The mother and daughter will draw closer together.[50]

A good way to create intimacy between parent and child, as well as to draw the child out, is to ask on the way home from school, or in the evening, "What was your favorite thing that happened today? What was your least favorite?" Listen for conclusions being made and watch for errors in processing the day's events. Ask gentle questions to help the child figure it all out, to develop sound core and mid-level evaluations. Nothing should be off the table for discussion. One-on-one time between each parent and each child can go a long way toward communicating, "I enjoy being with you."

Relating stories about oneself as a child makes you, the adult, warm, friendly, and approachable. Children, then, are more likely to open up. For example, "I messed my pants in school when I was your age and felt awful and embarrassed like something was really wrong with me. No one would come near me, but when I got home, mom cleaned me up, put me in a fresh set of clothes, and sent me outside to play. I felt better." After such stories—not just one—children will begin to speak with increased ease. When adults begin thinking about their own childhoods as an aid to the young, stories may start flowing, though again the adults must not be didactic or moralistic in their discussions. Adults must feel both love and empathy toward their charges and express genuine concern in a believable way.

Donna Bryant Goertz, Montessori teacher in an early elementary school (ages 6 to 9), gives a striking example of the contrast between two adult personalities in handling a potentially serious situation.[51] A girl, Dagmar, in one class sent a letter, supposedly signed by a few boys, saying the boys will beat up Lila, a girl in Goertz's class, if Lila goes near Dagmar. Goertz acknowledged Lila's emotions by saying, "Oh, a threatening letter. That could be scary." Lila immediately suspected Dagmar

---

[50] Ginott, *Between Parent & Child*, 23–24.
[51] Goertz, *Children Who Are Not Yet Peaceful*, chap. 15.

as the writer and said Dagmar is mad at her, but she also said the boys will not beat her up. Goertz told the other teacher and soon regretted it. The other teacher was an authoritarian personality who immediately confronted Dagmar. Just as immediately Dagmar denied the whole thing.

Goertz then had to work harder to draw Dagmar out. She talked caringly to Dagmar and slowly evoked a confession, but most importantly she elicited the reason why the letter was written in the first place. Goertz's comments to Dagmar ranged from "Lila got a scary letter. Probably somebody's feeling bad about writing it" to "If someone else put the boys' names on [the letter], that person could be feeling really bad" to "I wonder if you could help me make some of [the boys who wrote the letter] feel better" to "The person who wrote the letter must be really scared." At this point (with much omitted in my summary of the actual conversation), Dagmar admitted that she wrote the letter and that the boys knew nothing about it. So why are you so angry to have written such a letter was Goertz's next question. "[The boys] used to play only with me, and now whenever I go to my dad's they want us to play with [Lila] all the time." So said Goertz, "That could really hurt your feelings. . . . Could you tell Lila about your feelings?" The two then had a "very sweet and moving" conversation.

One upshot of this story is that Dagmar lied because she was afraid and wrote the threatening letter because she was hurt. With no one to talk to about her situation or feelings, Dagmar reacted in a not-so-nice way. Goertz, through her intervention, probably "caught in the making" a potentially negative core evaluation, plus the beginnings of one or more defensive habits. The authoritarian teacher's approach to handling Dagmar likely would have led to both. The other upshot of this and the other stories described above is that emotional communication to draw feelings out of young children requires great skill and tact. This includes an almost infinite patience and substantial creativity. The skill does not come naturally to most of us, but that is what is needed to teach introspection.

Conversations of the Ginott and Goertz style are probably the best way to communicate with children of all ages. Directly quizzing the young is often not effective or desirable, because some (or many) children may feel put on the spot, or may simply not be able to articulate what they are feeling and most certainly the evaluations underlying those feelings. This is where workbooks and worksheets, utilizing both writing and drawing, and perhaps even a journal, can come in handy. Unfortunately, no workbooks or worksheets to date exist that teach all of Packer's steps of introspection.

One example nonetheless that asks children to introspect on a limited scale is *My Quality World Workbook* by Carleen Glasser, and for older children Glasser's *The Quality World Activity Set*.[52] The quality world is William Glasser's concept of what we all aim to achieve in life, that is, the collection of people, things, and beliefs that will satisfy our needs and make us happy. If we are not happy and our world is not high in quality, something is not right in our selection of one or more of those people, things, and beliefs, which means the collection we do have is failing to meet our needs.[53] The Carleen Glasser workbooks are designed to encourage young children to think about the quality world that would make them happy and the steps to, or means of, achieving those goals.

Another example that is closer to Packer's theory is the set of worksheets and other materials developed by cognitive behavior therapist Woody Schuldt. The materials can be found on his website www.therapistaid.com. The worksheets are designed for mental health professionals but some, perhaps many, can be adapted and used by parents and teachers. One worksheet consists of what Schuldt calls "printable emotion faces," drawings that express about twenty different emotions. Such a worksheet should be helpful to children who have difficulty articulating the emotions they are feeling. Other worksheets include "self-esteem sentence completion," "anger activity for children,"

---

[52] Carleen Glasser, *My Quality World Workbook* (Los Angeles: www.wglasserbooks. com, 2017) and *The Quality World Activity Set* (Los Angeles: wglasserbooks.com, 1996).

[53] Glasser, *Choice Theory*, 45. "People, things, and beliefs" are one's chosen values, though Glasser does not use the precise term "values."

and "goal sheet," among about forty others. The website is extensive with additional interactive tools, guides, and articles. It can be filtered by demographic (children, adolescents, or adults) and by topic.[54]

Similar materials, geared specifically to Packer's steps of introspecting emotions, need to be developed.[55] Content should focus on the following questions, though for the very young the materials most likely should not be so explicit.[56] In the identification steps, it is important to make clear, as Packer puts it simply, "When [a child] feels something, he's really thinking something."[57] Thus: What do you feel? What thoughts were going through your mind when you felt the emotion? What would the emotion say if it could talk? What happened—what facts of the situation occurred—when you felt the emotion? "Universal and personal evaluations" are not something we would expect the young to understand, but they know when someone has been unfair to them, when they feel bad or hurt, or when they feel danger or afraid.

Assessing the evaluations would come next: Does what the emotion is saying reflect the truth about what happened in the situation? Are what the emotion is saying and the thoughts going through your mind good thoughts or bad thoughts about you, other people, and the world you live in? Are the good thoughts really good or do you just feel like they are good? Might they be not so good? Are the bad thoughts really bad or do you just feel like they are bad? Might they be not so bad? If the underlying evaluations are valid, the materials (and adults) should indicate that there is no need to continue.

---

[54] Schuldt's site includes the disclaimer that these worksheets are intended only for professionals and do not replace therapy. Parents and teachers, with careful examination, should be able to use them. Cognitive behavior therapy is close to Packer's approach to psychology and therapy, but it is not the same.

[55] Other workbooks and worksheets for children do exist on the market, but cautious judgment must be exercised before deciding to use them, adapting them to one's own children and students.

[56] Ginott and Goertz demonstrate to us how to talk to children without cross-examining them; workbook and worksheet materials, one would hope, would follow the same pattern.

[57] Edith Packer, "Interview with Edith Packer," 278.

Identifying reasons for experiencing a current emotion is challenging: Why do you think you felt that emotion? What might a different emotion say in the same situation that would make you feel different about yourself, other people, and the world? The emphasis on self, others, and the world is aiming to identify core evaluations. The last step requires practice, so these questions should ask: How might you change what you say to yourself that would change your emotion? What can you do to practice this new way of thinking?

Young children (and many adults) have difficulty naming their emotions and may instead describe facts or concretes of the situation in which the event occurs. Or they may name the emotion but cannot remember the specifics of the event. The concretes are what give rise to the personal evaluation, so this should not be looked at as a problem, and the emotion includes the concretes though the child (or adult) may not be aware of them. Talking warmly to a child or adult in the Ginott or Goertz style can gradually bring out the needed emotion or concretes.[58]

The next to last step of introspection—identifying reasons for the mistaken evaluations—is the most difficult, because it involves core and mid-level evaluations, as well as ingrained defensive habits. It is here that some may require professional help. Adults, such as parents and teachers, who are not professional psychologists may still be able to benefit children and adolescents as lay helpers. Elementary questions about what the young feel about themselves, others, and the world, with carefully worded, probing questions about defensive habits, can draw mistaken conclusions out. In this way, adults can help the young make corrections.

We feel what we feel, and so do young children and adolescents. Emotions of the young must be taken seriously by adults. The cause of emotions has been programmed by us as they are automatized reactions to objects, persons, or events. Our emotions may seem unchangeable,

---

[58]Judith Beck's short chapter on identifying emotions, which covers this issue, provides helpful approaches in the tradition of cognitive behavior therapy. Beck, *Cognitive Behavior Therapy*, chap. 10.

but the point of introspection is to catch inappropriate emotions in the making or otherwise to correct the ones that have become entrenched habits.

In the not too distant future, one can hope that parents and teachers become skilled sufficiently in introspection and the teaching of introspection such that we all become aware of our core and mid-level evaluations and the causes of our emotions. Or, if we do not immediately know them, we know how to access and identify them. It is this skill that is essential to the development and maintenance of independence and independent judgment.

THE SKILLS OF HAPPINESS

Happiness is an emotion that results from the achievement of our chosen, objectively valid, rational values. It does not result from lying and cheating or from whining and complaining or from mooching off others and manipulating them. Nor does it result from alcohol or drugs. Nor does it necessarily result from skydiving three times a week or from attending frequent parties, both of which are rational values but also could be defenses. Like all emotions, happiness is made possible by the evaluations we have made and the way we hold those evaluations in our minds.

Happiness results from a life of reason, which means a commitment to honesty, integrity, and productive work. It means a commitment to facts—about ourselves, including our psychologies, facts about other people, and facts about the world in which we live. It means that each one of us alone must identify and judge the facts according to rigorous logic. It means that we must exert effort and take action to achieve our values and not be intimidated into silence or inaction by a nonobjective fear or swayed by the irrational opinions or demands of others.

Happiness is a consequence of psychological independence and independent judgment. As such, it is both a skill that derives from a life of introspective competence and an outcome of that competence. Experiencing happiness does not mean that we never suffer misfortune, tragedy, or other obstacles to success in life. It means we have correct attitudes on how to handle misfortune and, in due time, move on to other values that will continue our state of happiness.[59] Teaching psychological independence to children and adolescents, therefore, means teaching the skills required for happiness. Prerequisite in both parents and teachers is the conviction that happiness is a birthright for everyone.

The most essential skill of happiness is the development from childhood of correct core and mid-level evaluations, in particular the judgment that one's own life and values are important, regardless of what anyone else might say or think. This means a commitment not just to independence, but also to egoism. Children, as Packer points out, are "complete egoists" who often can successfully entertain themselves while alone. In this sense, similar to the "aloneness of independence," there is also an "aloneness to happiness," meaning it is we alone, each one of us, who must choose and pursue the values that will make us happy. Because our culture today is a culture of self-sacrifice and psychological dependence, many parents and teachers work hard to destroy the child's natural pursuit of self-interested values.[60] To become a happy person, the child must learn, and be allowed and encouraged to develop, several competencies for making oneself happy.

Packer identifies four such competencies. The first one is the already mentioned skill of making oneself happy while alone, whether it be reading, listening to music, or putting puzzles together. The ability to entertain oneself while alone emphasizes the significance that just as no one can do our thinking for us, no one can identify values for us to give us a genuine pleasure. We each alone are in control of and responsible for our lives. We are the best judge of what and what not to value. This includes our most important values of career and romantic partner. We can consult others for advice, consider their opinions, and accumulate knowledge, but in the end we must make

---

[59] On the handling of misfortune, see Paul McHugh's discussion of the emotions of adjustment—grief, homesickness, demoralization due to rivalry or jealousy, and post-traumatic stress—especially, their similarities. McHugh, *Try to Remember*, 183.

[60] Packer, "Happiness Skills," 67–70. Egoism, of course, means neither sacrificing oneself to others nor others to oneself.

first-handed decisions and take first-handed actions to make ourselves happy.[61] Second-handedness—letting others choose our values for us—is not a path to happiness.

The complete egoist, says Packer, in addition to being comfortable when alone, is committed to exerting effort and taking action. Effort and action are two competencies that are related but emphasize different components of the required skills. Effort means work, directing mental and physical energy to the achievement of a goal, whether it is learning to ride a bicycle or to understand and use the quadratic equation. Both learning and practice, that is, the acquisition of knowledge and its application, require directed energy to produce results that, in turn, can, and should, produce pleasure—if parents and teachers have not turned the effort into drudgery or a sacrificial duty. In this way, if left free to direct one's energy to pursue one's values, the child learns an important connection between work and happiness. Effort, or work, is the key to achieving values and achieved values are what make us happy. Thus, freely and independently chosen effort becomes the pleasureful pursuit of happiness.[62]

Action is the process of exerting that effort, actual movement toward the goal, not daydreams or fantasies about what one is going to do someday. Packer includes this skill to emphasize the need to act to make oneself happy. Happiness cannot and does not result from delay or procrastination. The happy person, Packer insists, says, "I can and I will" achieve my values, not "I will try." The happy person acts, confident that he or she can and will overcome obstacles in the pursuit of values, not complaining about problems, but enjoying the process of finding solutions. And the happy person acts, not just in the physical or behavioral sense, but also, and more importantly, in the mental sense of acting to understand one's psychology, expanding one's knowledge and understanding of work, and applying "reason and logic to everything that is relevant to his life."[63]

---

[61]Packer, "Happiness Skills," 70–72.
[62]Packer, "Happiness Skills," 72–73.
[63]Packer, "Happiness Skills," 74–75.

Commitment to acting against—but not repressing—negative emotions, especially fear, is the fourth competency we need to achieve happiness successfully. Letting these emotions stop us prevents us from exploring different values to see which ones we want to hold onto and make a part of our personal identity. Succumbing to fear as a child can lead to a constricted life as an adult, and such adults, as Packer puts it, become "slaves to their fears." Often, it is a fear of failure. The child who cannot muster the courage to say no to a schoolyard bully may become the adult who cannot take the risk of leaving a boring, unchallenging job. The antidote to fear, says Packer, is thinking, because thought is the source and cause of our emotions. Identifying the causes of our unrealistic, psychological fears clears the path to our goals. This, in turn, makes it possible for us to act—and, again, we must choose to act because the unrealistic fear will still be present.[64]

The fundamental happiness skill underlying all of the above is the uncompromising commitment to facts. This brings independence and happiness together, for a strict adherence to facts without regard for one's—or others'—irrational wishes, hopes, or fears creates both the independent personality and, by producing an unobstructed path to the achievement of one's values, happiness. "The happy person," says Packer, "always asks whether or not he can change a fact that he dislikes. He does not fight unchangeable reality. . . . [And] he does not try to fool himself by thinking he can feel good in defiance of facts." The happy person, in other words, does not argue with the fact that there are only twenty-four hours in a day or that he or she is only five feet tall. The happy person "does not make exceptions to the acceptance of facts."[65]

To emphasize, the pursuer of first-handed values in strict accordance with the facts is not boring. The happy person, to conclude Packer's thoughts, "milks his values," possesses a "positive magnet," and in the

---

[64]Packer, "Happiness Skills," 76–79.

[65]Packer, "Happiness Skills," 79–83. Underlying this statement is Ayn Rand's distinction between the metaphysical and the man-made, between "facts I cannot change" and "facts I can change." Rand, "Metaphysical Versus the Man-Made," 32–33 and throughout.

end is like a child in a toy store. Milking a value means exerting additional effort to enjoy it, such as playing a new recording over and over until it is almost memorized or researching the singers or band fully to understand who they are and where they came from.[66] A positive magnet means that the cup is often or nearly always half full, instead of half empty. To the happy person, the world is fun, not dangerous or malevolent.[67]

"The happy person," says Packer, "is like a child with lots of money in his pocket who finds himself in a toy store chock full of values he can select, because he can afford them. His desire for values has no limit."[68]

THE FUTURE OF PSYCHOLOGY

Thinking errors are the root of psychological problems. Correct thinking in all areas of our lives is the root not just of psychological health, but also of independence and happiness. The emphasis on correct thinking and thinking errors indicates the direction of future research in psychology. It also indicates how the research must be conducted.

The challenge of psychology is that hundreds, perhaps thousands or millions, of thoughts over the course of a lifetime determine our emotions and behavior. Probably hundreds of thoughts go through our minds in a single day. The thoughts may not differ from hour to hour or day to day, but repetitive, internal deliberations determine what we will express and do externally. Some thoughts we may want to keep hidden in our minds, in our subconscious, but those are the thinking errors that can and should be corrected with introspection. Defensive habits often do not cooperate with our conscious desire to keep certain thoughts and behaviors unknown, unfelt, or unexpressed. They may come out without our permission. Only correction of those thoughts will remove the subconscious and conscious conflicts that prevent us from experiencing genuine independence and happiness.

---

[66] Packer, "Happiness Skills," 84–85, 89. Cf. Montessori on the significance of repetition. Montessori, *Montessori Method*, 357–58.

[67] Packer, "Happiness Skills," 66.

[68] Packer, "Happiness Skills," 83

Scientific research in psychology requires the method of conceptualization used by Freud, which is the same method used by Jane Goodall in biology. The uniqueness of observation in psychology is that it requires conversation with others to identify universal concepts of the field, such as repression and the other defensive habits. In particular, advances in psychology of the future will depend on further discovery of how these mental habits are formed and changed, that is, how our conscious and subconscious minds interact and how our introspective competence can be improved in both efficiency and effectiveness to identify and correct those interactions to better direct and control our lives.

This last is the specialized field of psycho-epistemology, the study of the methods of using our minds, sometimes referred to as the psychology of thinking. It has barely begun to be researched. If it is studied in earnest, using a more correct epistemology, and if enough of us are consequently able to develop and maintain an independent and happy life, we will eagerly strive to support and maintain our free society.

The newest, unexplored frontier of science is not just outer space, but that objective reality called our conscious and subconscious minds.

Appendix

A Note on Freud, the Subconscious, and Repression

"Its intention [psychoanalysis] . . . ," says Freud, "is to strengthen the ego, to make it more independent of the super-ego, to widen its field of perception and enlarge its organization, so that it can appropriate fresh portions of the id. Where id was, there ego shall be. It is a work of culture—not unlike the draining of the Zuider Zee."[1]

I submit that this quotation sums up Freud's contribution to and influence on subsequent psychology, including a significant influence on those psychologists who consider psychoanalysis "pseudoscience" and never, or rarely, mention in their own work such concepts as the sub- (or un-) conscious, introspection, or repression.[2]

The quotation from Freud contains three insights. Reworded in contemporary language, using the principles of Edith Packer, the aim of psychology is (1) to correct and reinforce our conscious and subconscious premises to make us more independent of internal and external influences, (2) by making, insofar as possible, our subconscious

---

[1] Freud, *New Introductory Lectures*, 99–100. The Zuiderzee was a large bay in northwestern Netherlands that, beginning in 1920, was turned into a fresh water lake with nearly 600 square miles of reclaimed land.

[2] Nor, for that matter, free will, though Freud, as a determinist, would not have used those words either.

conscious, to give us better control of our lives, and (3) to reclaim—a word used in one translation of the Freud passage—and build on the assets we already possess.[3]

"Where subconscious, mistaken conclusions were," one might update Freud, "there confident and independent self-assertion shall guide." The unstated premise of the quotation from Freud is that if we don't take control of our conscious and subconscious lives, our subconscious will prevail.

Philosopher Richard Wollheim further identifies Freud's legacy to later psychologists as the removal of "symptoms of a mental disorder through the use of words," that is, talk therapy, and the removal of disorders by tracing them back "to the influence of ideas," which is to say that Freud's psychology, deriving from his work on hysteria, is *ideogenic*, asserting that psychological problems are *idea-made*. Attached to the ideas are affects (or emotions). Freud's recognition of this connection, says Wollheim, probably stems from the influence of Aristotelian philosopher Franz Brentano at the University of Vienna, where Freud was Brentano's student.[4]

Lancelot Law Whyte in his 1960 book *The Unconscious before Freud* traces the history of the concept of un- (or sub-) conscious mental contents and processes. His definition of "unconscious" is broad enough to include "subconscious" and also to include, or not include, Freud's id. Whyte's history ranges from Galen in the second century AD to the mid-twentieth, though most of his efforts are spent on the discovery of the unconscious from about 1680 to 1880. Whyte concludes that Freud obliged us "to face the problem of finding an adequate concept of the unconscious mind," by showing us, "once and for all, that the unconscious is so powerful that this task cannot be neglected."[5]

---

[3] "It is reclamation work, like the draining of the Zuyder Zee." Sigmund Freud, *New Introductory Lectures on Psycho-Analysis*, trans. W. J. H. Sprott (New York: Carlton House, 1933), 112.

[4] Richard Wollheim, *Sigmund Freud* (Cambridge, UK: Cambridge University Press, 1971), xi, 19–20.

[5] Lancelot Law Whyte, *The Unconscious before Freud: A History of the Evolution of Human Awareness* (New York: Basic Books, 1960), 10. Whyte's definition of the

Unfortunately, many, if not most, non-Freudian psychologists today fail to do just that. They neglect, by neither studying nor mentioning, those "mental factors which are not directly available to our awareness [that] influence both our behavior and the conscious aspect of our thought."[6]

The significance of the discovery of a sub- or unconscious mind, says Whyte, is that it was a "first correction" to Descartes' "blunder" of severing mind from body. The concept of a sub- or unconscious mind brings consciousness and existence together as a unified whole of mind, brain, and body. Consciousness is an active process that perceives existence, exhibiting various levels of awareness some of which we are not at the moment fully attending to. Those levels of awareness below focused attention extend down to the integrating and generalizing actions of our brains that we infer from the brain's products.[7]

This point raises the further questions: Are we talking about a "sub-" or "un-" conscious? And how precisely does it operate?[8]

The concept and word "unconscious" means "not conscious," whereas "subconscious" means "below or beneath consciousness." Because consciousness is both the faculty and state of awareness, we can also say "not aware" for unconscious or "below or beneath

---

unconscious: "all mental factors and processes of which we are not immediately aware, whatever they be." Whyte, *Unconscious before Freud*, 21. Many, though not all, in Whyte's survey describe an unconscious similar to Freud's, namely as a powerful seat of demons and will that influence and control us. The subconscious, properly understood, however, controls us only because we have empowered it with mistaken conclusions.

[6] Whyte, *Unconscious before Freud*, 18.

[7] Whyte, *Unconscious before Freud*, 26. Descartes' "blunder" or "error," as it is sometimes called, can in contrast to the conventional view be understood as an advance (though a confused one). Descartes in effect brought the "consciousness in the sky" (the Christian God) down to earth, by putting it in our bodies and making it personal to each one of us. This was a first move away from mysticism. (I am indebted to my wife, Linda Reardan, for this observation, based on her study of recent Cartesian scholars.)

[8] And "do we possess free will?" is not one of the questions, as determinism, again, is victim of the self-excepting fallacy.

awareness" for subconscious.[9] Freud rejected the latter because he thought it was confusing, referring either to a location "topographically" beneath consciousness or to a separate, "qualitatively" different or "subterranean" consciousness.[10] Freud required a concept of the "not conscious" because, according to his theory, much that we are not aware of in the unconscious is also not ever accessible to us, such as the processes of the id, home of our alleged inborn primitive drives, impulses, and untamed passions. However, if there are no inborn demons or will that we are not directly aware of, there is no need for such a concept as the unconscious.

The notion of an unconscious, in addition, is itself ambiguous because there are many, many things we are not aware of, including the circulation of our blood and most of the rest of the universe. Below or beneath awareness, to be sure, is a metaphor from the physical world, but so are most of the other concepts we use to describe consciousness and its processes. By talking about "beneath awareness," we mean there are several levels or degrees of consciousness.

At the "top" level, to use one more metaphor, there is the completely aware state, say, of the intense conversation mentioned earlier while driving, along with the learned habit of driving a car and the standing order to drive defensively.[11] We are less explicitly aware of habits and standing orders, such as those involved in driving, because the routine thoughts and actions required to drive were long ago automatized, though in the present we are sufficiently aware of how to use those thoughts and actions to drive and to be alert to other cars on the road. In the event of an emergency, assuming good driving habits have been formed, certain thoughts and actions can immediately be called to the forefront of consciousness, for example, to stop quickly or change lanes.

---

[9] Branden, *Psychology of Self-Esteem*, 5–8. "Faculty," in the Aristotelian sense, Branden emphasizes, means "power or ability."

[10] Sigmund Freud, *The Question of Lay Analysis*, trans. and ed. James Strachey (New York: W. W. Norton, 1978), 19. First published in German in 1926.

[11] See above, pp. 89–90.

What has been automatized—and this includes the extensive accumulated knowledge that we are not now using—is stored in lower levels of consciousness that we call the subconscious. Below awareness, yes, but not *un-* conscious in the sense of being unknowable or inaccessible. Learning of any kind, whether that of a skill like driving or complex concepts like epistemology and psychology, is an act, first, of volitionally focused, concentrated attention. In this act of the acquisition of concepts we identify facts and make evaluations, connections, and differentiations. Then, through application or practice, which last means repetition, we program, that is, give instructions to, the subconscious to integrate and automatize the new material, forming cognitive habits and, as appropriate, physical skills. We consciously give the instructions, the subconscious integrates and automatizes.

The child, for example, who has learned, through repeated experiences, to distinguish two four-legged animals, say dogs and cats, has successfully processed and automatized their differences, though probably not in precise wording, as perceptual concretes do not require such explicitness. The child nonetheless has formed two concepts that are stored in the subconscious and are available for recall the next time a trigger—the perception of similar animals—presents itself.

All learning, including especially the evaluations—core, mid-level, and concrete—that determine our psychologies, follows this pattern that begins at the conscious, volitional level, subsequently programming our subconscious. The better the programming, the better our subconscious content and processes will be organized and will operate rationally, the greater the ease and accuracy with which we will be able to recall and use the stored, previously learned knowledge and values, and the more appropriate, that is, rational, our reactions will be to the people, things, and events we experience in the present. Mistaken stored conclusions, or worse, failure to take volitional control of our conscious programming due to evasion or laziness or lack of education on how to take such control is what gives us a messed up subconscious, meaning psychological problems and possibly a bad character.[12]

The subconscious, to emphasize, is not identical to memory, nor is it correct to call consciousness solely an "information processor," which is an incomplete and superficial, jargon-filled metaphor. The subconscious includes content and processes that we are not currently aware of, but we can access both with the right technique. Content includes memories, which if defined broadly can include the acquired knowledge and evaluations that underlie and cause our emotions and guide our actions.[13] What is more significant about the subconscious, as Freud recognized, is its processes.

Like consciousness, the subconscious is a dynamic, active process in the sense that it is an integrating and generalizing activity. It acts whether we choose to control it or not. And we know this because of the nature of dreams, creative insight, and repression. Connections, which we may not always like or appreciate, are made when we are asleep, when we are not in conscious control. Sleep nonetheless is a lower level of awareness, so it is incorrect to say we are "unconscious" when in dreamland. We know sleep is subconscious because sounds in the night can sometimes be incorporated into our dreams. We remain aware on some level.

Creative insight—the "aha" solution to a problem that comes to mind seemingly involuntarily—is also a connection made by the subconscious. This occurs because innovators, writers, and problem solvers in general accumulate huge contexts surrounding what they are working on and give themselves standing orders to be aware of anything that may be relevant to the problem under study. The "aha" insight may occur while taking a walk, playing solitaire, when first

---

[12] The above paragraph, once again, describes the undeveloped and unstudied field of psycho-epistemology, science of the methods—both good and bad—by which we use our minds, including in particular the interactions between conscious and subconscious processes. See Rand, "Philosophy: Who Needs It," in *Philosophy: Who Needs It*, 7–8, and Rand, "The Comprachicos," 192–94.

[13] Memory, properly understood, is the faculty (power or ability) of preserving and recalling thoughts, emotions, and experiences.

waking up in the morning, or while working on the problem. Why? Because the subconscious is making connections no matter what we are doing. Creative people learn to program their subconscious minds for best use.

In this sense, the subconscious, as Whyte said above but now restated in the positive, becomes "so powerful that this task [the study of the subconscious] cannot be neglected."

Repression is the exact opposite of the creative process. We tell ourselves, "I don't want to feel that," and we often become successful in varying degrees of not feeling certain emotions, or much of them. The aim of repression is to mute the experience of emotions. Thus, through an initial order to hinder or bar one emotion, repressive integration and generalization can spread to many, and in some cases, most emotions. The word "mute" means to diminish the feeling's intensity or to prevent its experience entirely. The process works as a standing order not to feel when perceiving a triggering object, person, or event. When repression is uncorrected, more connections and generalizations of a negative kind will continue to be made, which will cause us a considerable unhappiness.

If paying attention, meaning introspecting, we can sometimes know repression is operating because of behavioral reactions. Our shy young man from chapters 3 and 5, for example, upon seeing an attractive woman at a party may immediately find his eyes darting away from her and perhaps even experience a twitch of his head to the side such that the woman concludes he is not interested in talking to her. Thorough introspection, and perhaps therapy, may reveal subconsciously repressed core and mid-level evaluations that undercut the young man's desire to meet and date a member of the opposite sex. The repression has likely diminished or prevented the young man's awareness of self-doubt and feelings of unworthiness in social situations, but the resulting overwhelming anxiety has also likely led to his crippling behavior.[14]

---

[14] See above, pp. 94–95, 155–56, 159.

Not all repression produces overt behavioral reactions, but if we are monitoring what goes through our minds in situations we have identified as repression-triggering occasions, we can learn to slow down our thinking sufficiently to be aware of the evaluations producing the unwanted emotions.

Repressed material is there, in our subconscious, and is accessible. The subconscious is not our id, or a "chaos" or "cauldron full of seething excitations," unless we have created it to be that way. The subconscious most importantly includes the conclusions we have drawn about life events. These conclusions have formed our psychologies and have determined whether or not we will be happy. Repression is a real, subconscious process that begins at the conscious, volitional level.

Introspection is required to discover repression's effects and causes and is the means of remedying those ill effects and maintaining good mental health, which includes psychological independence.

Bibliography

Ansbacher, Heinz L., and Rowena R. Ansbacher, eds., *The Individual Psychology of Alfred Adler: A Systematic Presentation in Selections from His Writings*. New York: Harper Torchbook, 1964.

Arieti, Silvano. *Interpretation of Schizophrenia*, 2nd ed. New York: Basic Books, 1974. First edition published in 1955.

Asch, S. E. "Effects of Group Pressure upon the Modification and Distortion of Judgments," 2–11. In *Readings in Social Psychology*. New York: Henry Holt, 1952.

———. "Studies of Independence and Conformity." *Psychological Monographs: General and Applied* 70, no. 9 (1956): 1–70.

Ashton, T. S., *The Industrial Revolution: 1750–1840*. Rev. ed. London: Oxford University Press, 1969. First published in 1948.

"Augustine of Hippo," *Wikiquote*. Last modified January 29, 2019. https://en.wikiquote.org/wiki/Augustine_of_Hippo.

Barton, Adriana. "Study Renews Debate about Surgical Treatment for Psychiatric Disorders." *The Globe and Mail*, June 6, 2013. https://www.theglobeandmail.com/.

Beck, Aaron. "Thinking and Depression." *Archives of General Psychiatry* 9, no. 10 (October 1963): 324–33.

———. "Thinking and Depression II: Theory and Therapy." *Archives of General Psychiatry* 10, no. 6 (June 1964): 561–71.

Beck, Judith S. *Cognitive Behavior Therapy: Basics and Beyond*, 2nd ed. New York: Guilford Press, 2011. First edition published in 1995.

Bentall, Richard P. *Madness Explained: Psychosis and Human Nature*. London: Penguin Books, 2003.

Bettelheim, Bruno. *Freud and Man's Soul*. New York: Vintage Books, 1984.

Blumenthal, Allan. *Identity, Inner Life and Psychological Change*. Self-published, CreateSpace, 2013.

Bowlby, John. *Maternal Care and Mental Health*. Geneva: World Health Organization, 1951.

Branden, Barbara. "A Biographical Essay: Who Is Ayn Rand?" In Nathaniel Branden, *Who Is Ayn Rand*, 149–239. New York: Random House, 1962.

———. "Efficient Thinking." In Nathaniel Branden, *The Vision of Ayn Rand: The Basic Principles of Objectivism*, chap. 6. Gilbert, ZA, Cobden Press, 2009.

———. *Think as if Your Life Depends on It: Principles of Efficient Thinking & Other Lectures*. Published by the author's estate, CreateSpace, 2017. Chapters 1-10 a transcription of ten-lecture series offered in the early 1960s.

Branden, Nathaniel. *The Disowned Self*. New York: Bantam Books, 1973.

———. *The Psychology of Self-Esteem: A Revolutionary Approach to Self-Understanding that Launched a New Era in Modern Psychology*. San Francisco: Jossey-Bass, 2001. First published in 1969 with the subtitle: *A New Concept of Man's Psychological Nature*.

———. *Six Pillars of Self-Esteem*. New York: Bantam, 1994.

———. *The Vision of Ayn Rand: The Basic Principles of Objectivism*. Gilbert, AZ: Cobden Press, 2009. Transcription of twenty-lecture series offered between 1958 and 1968.

Breggin, Peter R. "Alert 22: Threatening to 'Get Breggin!'" *Psychiatric Drug Facts*. Accessed February 8, 2019. https://breggin.com/alert-22-threatening-to-get-breggin/.

———. "The Fort Hood Shooter: A Different Psychiatric Perspective." *Huffpost Politics*, May 25, 2011. https://www.huffingtonpost.com/dr-peter-breggin/the-fort-hood-shooter-a-d_b_349651.html.

———. "Psychiatry's Role in the Holocaust." *International Journal of Risk & Safety in Medicine* 4, no. 2 (1993): 133–48.

———. *The Psychology of Freedom: Liberty and Love as a Way of Life*. Buffalo: Prometheus Books, 1980.

———. *Toxic Psychiatry: Why Therapy, Empathy, and Love Must Replace the Drugs, Electroshock, and Biochemical Theories of the "New Psychiatry."* New York: St. Martin's Press, 1991.

Breggin, Peter R., and Ginger Ross Breggin. "The Hazards of Treating 'Attention-Deficit/Hyperactivity Disorder' with Methylphenidate (Ritalin)." *Journal of College Student Psychotherapy* 10, no. 2 (1995): 55–72.

Browning, Christopher R. "Revisiting the Holocaust Perpetrators: Why Did They Kill?" lecture, University of North Carolina, Chapel Hill, NC, October 17, 2011. https://bhecinfo.org/wp-content/uploads/Revisiting-the-Holocaust-Perpetrators_Why-Did-They-Kill.pdf.

Childs, Jr., Roy A. "Big Business and the Rise of American Statism." In *Liberty Against Power: Essays by Roy A. Childs., Jr.*, edited by Joan Kennedy Taylor, 15–47. New York: Fox & Wilkes, 1994. First published in 1971 in *Reason* magazine, with subsequent revision.

Chirkov, Valery, Richard M. Ryan, Youngmee Kim, and Ulas Kaplan. "Differentiating Autonomy From Individualism and Independence: A Self-Determination Theory Perspective on Internalization of Cultural Orientations and Well-Being." *Journal of Personality and Social Psychology* 84, no. 1 (2003): 97–110.

Deci, Edward L., and Richard Flaste. *Why We Do What We Do: Understanding Self-Motivation*. New York: Penguin Books, 1995.

deMause, Lloyd. "The Evolution of Childhood." In *The History of Childhood: The Untold Story of Child Abuse*," edited by Lloyd deMause, 1–73. New York: Peter Bedrick Books, 1988. First published in 1974.

———. "On Writing Childhood History." *Journal of Psychohistory* 16, no. 2 (Fall 1988): 135–70.

Dewey, John. *Experience and Nature*, 2nd ed. Chicago: Open Court, 1929. First edition published in 1925.

Doidge, Norman. *The Brain That Changes Itself: Stories of Personal Triumph from the Frontiers of Brain Science*. New York: Viking Penguin, 2007.

Domarus, E. von. "The Specific Laws of Thought in Schizophrenia." In *Language and Thought in Schizophrenia*, edited by J. S. Kasanin, 104–14. Berkeley: University of California Press, 1944.

Dreikurs, Rudolf. "The Private Logic." In *Alfred Adler: His Influence on Psychology Today*, edited by Harold H. Mosak, 19–32. Park Ridge, NJ: Noyes Press, 1973.

Dweck, Carol. *Mindset: The New Psychology of Success*. New York: Ballantine Books, 2008.

Ellis, Albert. "Rational Psychotherapy and Individual Psychology." *Journal of Individual Psychology* 13, no. 1 (1957): 38–44.

Foucault, Michel. *Madness & Civilization: A History of Insanity in the Age of Reason*. Translated by Richard Howard. New York: Vintage Books, 1973. First published in French in 1964.

Frankl, Victor. *Man's Search for Meaning*. Boston: Beacon Press, 1959.

Freud, Anna. *The Ego and the Mechanisms of Defence*. Translated by Cecil Baines. New York: International Universities Press, 1946. First published in German in 1936.

Freud, Sigmund. *Inhibitions, Symptoms and Anxiety*. Translated by Alix Strachey. New York: W. W. Norton, 1959. First published in German in 1926.

———. *New Introductory Lectures on Psycho-Analysis*. Translated and edited by James Strachey. New York: W. W. Norton, 1965. First published in German in 1933. First English translation by W. J. H. Sprott. New York: Carlton House, 1933.

———. *The Question of Lay Analysis*. Translated and edited by James Strachey. New York: W. W. Norton, 1978. First published in German in 1926.

Friedan, Betty. *The Feminine Mystique*. New York: W.W. Norton, 1963.

Gay, Peter. *Freud for Historians*. New York: Oxford University Press, 1985.

———. *Freud: A Life for Our Time*. New York: W. W. Norton, 1988.

Ginnott, Haim G. *Between Parent & Child: New Solutions to Old Problems*. New York: Macmillan, 1965.

———. *Teacher and Child: A Book for Parents and Teachers*. New York: Collier Books, 1972.

Glasser, Carleen. *My Quality World Workbook*. Los Angeles: www.wglasserbooks .com, 2017.

———. *The Quality World Activity Set*. Los Angeles: wglasserbooks.com, 1996.

Glasser, William. *Choice Theory: A New Psychology of Personal Freedom*. New York: HarperPerennial, 1999.

———. *Positive Addiction*. New York: Harper Perennial, 1985. First published in 1976.

———. *Reality Therapy: A New Approach to Psychiatry.* New York: Harper & Row Perennial Library, 1990. First published in 1965.

———. *Unhappy Teenagers: A Way for Parents and Teachers to Reach Them.* New York: HarperCollins, 2002.

Global Initiative to End All Corporal Punishment. Accessed February 8, 2019. https://www.endcorporalpunishment.org/countdown/.

Goertz, Donna Bryant. *Children Who Are Not Yet Peaceful: Preventing Exclusion in the Early Elementary Classroom.* Berkeley, CA: Frog Books, 2001.

Goodall, Jane. *In the Shadow of Man.* New York: Mariner Books, 2000. First published in 1971.

Gordon, Thomas. *Parent Effectiveness Training: The Tested Way to Raise Responsible Children.* New York: Three Rivers Press, 2000. First published in 1970.

Greenberg Daniel. *The Crisis in American Education.* Framingham, MA: Sudbury Valley School Press, 1970.

———. *Free at Last: The Sudbury Valley School.* Framingham, MA: Sudbury Valley School Press, 1987.

Hayek, F. A. *The Road to Serfdom: A Classic Warning Against the Dangers to Freedom Inherent in Social Planning.* Chicago: University of Chicago Press, 1944.

———. *The Counter-Revolution of Science: Studies on the Abuse of Reason*, 2nd ed. Indianapolis: Liberty*Press*, 1979. First edition published in 1952.

———., ed. *Capitalism and the Historians.* Chicago: University of Chicago Press, 1954.

Heywood, Colin. *A History of Childhood: Children and Childhood in the West from Medieval to Modern Times.* Cambridge, UK: Polity Press, 2001.

Hobbes, Thomas. *Leviathan or the Matter, Forme, & Power of a Common-wealth Ecclesiasticall and Civill.* London: Andrew Crooke, 1651.

Holmes, David S. "The Evidence for Repression: An Examination of Sixty Years of Research." In *Repression and Dissociation: Implications for Personality Theory, Psychopathology, and Health*, edited by Jerome L. Singer, 85–102. Chicago: University of Chicago Press, 1990.

Horney, Karen. *Neurosis and Human Growth: The Struggle toward Self-Realization.* New York: W. W. Norton, 1950.

Hurlburt, Russell T. *Investigating Pristine Inner Experience: Moments of Truth.* New York: Cambridge University Press, 2011.

Joseph, Jay. "'Bewitching Science' Revisited: Tales of Reunited Twins and the Genetics of Behavior." *Mad in America: Science, Psychiatry and Social Justice* (blog), March 16, 2016. https://www.madinamerica.com/category/blogs/. Search blog title.

———. *The Gene Illusion: Genetic Research in Psychiatry and Psychology Under the Microscope.* New York: Algora Publishing, 2004.

———. "Has a New Twin Study Meta-Analysis Finally 'Settled' the Nature-Nurture Debate?" *Mad in America: Science, Psychiatry and Social Justice* (blog), June 1, 2015. https://www.madinamerica.com/category/blogs/. Search blog title.

———. "The 1942 'Euthanasia' Debate in the *American Journal of Psychiatry*." *History of Psychiatry* 16, no. 2 (2005): 171–79. https://dx.doi.org/10.1177/0957154X05047004.

————. *Schizophrenia and Genetics: The End of an Illusion.* Self-published, Amazon Digital Services, 2017. Kindle.

————. "The Trouble with Twin Studies." *Mad in America: Science, Psychiatry and Social Justice* (blog), March 13, 2013. https://www.madinamerica.com /category/blogs/. Search blog title.

————. *The Trouble with Twin Studies: A Reassessment of Twin Research in the Social and Behavioral Sciences.* New York: Routledge, 2015.

Kant, Immanuel. *Critique of Pure Reason.* Translated and edited by Paul Guyer and Allen W. Wood. Cambridge, UK: Cambridge University Press, 1998. First published in German in 1781.

Kelley, David. *The Evidence of the Senses: A Realist Theory of Perception.* Baton Rouge, LA: Louisiana State University Press, 1986.

Kirkpatrick, Jerry. *In Defense of Advertising: Arguments from Reason, Ethical Egoism, and Laissez-Faire Capitalism.* Paperback ed. Claremont, CA: TLJ Books, 2007. First published in 1994.

————. *Montessori, Dewey, and Capitalism: Educational Theory for a Free Market in Education.* Claremont, CA: TLJ Books, 2008.

Kohn, Alfie. *Punished by Rewards: The Trouble with Gold Stars, Incentive Plans, A's, Praise, and Other Bribes.* Boston: Houghton Mifflin, 1993.

Lehrman, Daniel S. "A Critique of Konrad Lorenz's Theory of Instinctive Behavior." *The Quarterly Review of Biology* 28, no. 4 (December 1953): 337–63.

Leonard, Thomas C. "American Reform in the Progressive Era: Its Foundational Beliefs and Their Relation to Eugenics." *History of Political Economy* 41, no. 1 (2009): 109–41. https://dx.doi.org/10.1215/00182702-2008-040.

————. *Illiberal Reformers: Race, Eugenics and American Economics in the Progressive Era.* Princeton, NJ: Princeton University Press, 2016.

————. "Origins of the Myth of Social Darwinism: The Ambiguous Legacy of Richard Hofstadter's *Social Darwinism in American Thought.*" *Journal of Economic Behavior & Organization* 71 (2009): 37–51. https://doi .org/10.1016/j.jebo.2007.11.004.

Maslow, Abraham. "A Theory of Human Motivation." *Psychological Review* 50, no. 4 (1943): 370–96. https://dx.doi.org/10.1037/h0054346.

————. *Toward a Psychology of Being.* Blacksburg, VA: Wilder Publications, 2011. First published in 1962.

McCaskey, John P. "Induction in the Socratic Tradition." In *Shifting the Paradigm: Alternative Perspectives on Induction,* edited by Louis F. Groarke & Paolo C. Biondi, 161–92. Berlin: De Gruyter, 2014.

McHugh, Paul R. *The Mind Has Mountains: Reflections on Society and Psychiatry.* Baltimore: Johns Hopkins Press, 2006.

————. *Try to Remember: Psychiatry's Clash Over Meaning, Memory, and Mind.* New York: Dana Press, 2008.

Milgram, Stanley. *Obedience to Authority: An Experimental View.* New York: Harper Perennial, 1975.

Miller, Alice. *The Drama of the Gifted Child: The Search for the True Self.* Rev. ed. Translated by Ruth Ward. New York: Basic Books, 1997. First published in German in 1979.

——. *For Your Own Good: Hidden Cruelty in Child-Rearing and the Roots of Violence*. Translated by Hildegard and Hunter Hannum. New York: Farrar Straus Giroux, 1983. First Published in German in 1980.

——. "The Political Consequences of Child Abuse." *Journal of Psychohistory* 26, no. 2 (Fall 1998). http://psychohistory.com/articles/the-political -consequences-of-child-abuse/.

Miller, Arthur. *Arthur Miller's Adaptation of "An Enemy of the People" by Henrik Ibsen*. New York: Viking Penguin, 1951.

Mises, Ludwig von. *Bureaucracy*. New Haven: Yale University Press, 1944.

——. *Human Action: A Treatise on Economics*, 3rd rev. ed. Chicago: Henry Regnery, 1966. First published in German in 1940.

——. *Liberalism in the Classical Tradition*. Translated by Ralph Raico. William Volker Fund, 1962; reprint, San Francisco: Cobden Press, 1985. First published in German in 1927.

——. *Theory and History: An Interpretation of Social and Economic Evolution*. New Rochelle, NY: Arlington House, 1969.

Montessori, Maria. *The Absorbent Mind*. Translated by Claude A. Claremont. New York: Henry Holt, 1995. First published in Italian in 1949.

——. *The Montessori Method*. Translated by Anne E. George. New York: Schocken Books, 1964. First published in Italian in 1909.

——. *The Secret of Childhood*. Translated by M. Joseph Castelloe. New York: Ballantine Books, 1972. First published in Italian in 1936.

——. *Spontaneous Activity in Education*. Translated by Florence Simmonds. Cambridge, MA: Robert Bentley, 1971. First published in Italian in 1916.

Mounteer, Carl A. "Roman Childhood, 200 B.C. to A.D. 600." *Journal of Psychohistory* 14, no. 3 (Winter 1987): 233–56.

Mruk, Christopher J. *Self-Esteem Research, Theory, and Practice*, 3rd ed. New York: Springer Publishing, 2006. First edition published in 1995.

Nehamas, Alexander. "Pity and Fear in the *Rhetoric* and the *Poetics*." In *Essays on Aristotle's Poetics*, edited by Amélie Rorty, 291–314. Princteon, NJ: Princeton University Press, 1992.

Nicholls, Henry. "When I Met Jane Goodall, She Hugged Me Like a Chimp." *The Guardian*, April 3, 2014. https://www.theguardian.com/science /animal-magic/2014/apr/03/jane-goodall-80-chimp.

Nuland, Sherwin B. *The Doctors' Plague: Germs, Childbed Fever, and the Strange Story of Ignác Semmelweis*. New York: W. W. Norton, 2003.

Oliner, Samuel P., and Pearl M. Oliner. *The Altruistic Personality: Rescuers of Jews in Nazi Europe*. New York: Free Press, 1988.

Oppenheimer, Franz. *The State: Its History and Development Viewed Sociologically*. New York: Bobbs-Merrill, 1914.

Packer, Edith. *Lectures on Psychology: A Guide to Understanding Your Emotions*. Laguna Hills, CA: TJS Books, 2018. First published as Kindle e-book in 2012. Lectures delivered between 1983 and 1994. See esp. chap. 1, "Understanding the Subconscious"; chap. 3, "Happiness Skills"; chap. 4, "Anger"; chap. 6, "Toward a Lasting Romantic Relationship, Part II"; chap. 7, "The Role of Philosophy in Psychotherapy"; chap. 8, "The Art of Introspection"; and chap. 9, "The Psychological Requirements of a Free Society."

Peikoff, Leonard. "The Analytic-Synthetic Dichotomy." In Ayn Rand, *Introduction to Objectivist Epistemology*, expanded 2nd ed., 88–121. New York: NAL Books, 1990. First published in *The Objectivist*, May to September, 1967.

———. *Objectivism: The Philosophy of Ayn Rand*. New York: Penguin Books, 1991.

Pendergrast, Mark. *Memory Warp: How the Myth of Repressed Memory Arose and Refuses to Die*. Hinesburg, VT: Upper Access Books, 2017.

Perry, Bruce D., and Maia Szalavitz. *The Boy Who Was Raised as a Dog, and Other Stories from a Child Psychiatrist's Notebooks*. New York: Basic Books, 2006.

Popper, Karl. *Conjectures and Refutations*. New York: Routledge & Kegan Paul, 1963.

Porter, Roy. *Madness: A Brief History*. Oxford: Oxford University Press, 2001.

Rand, Ayn. *Atlas Shrugged*. New York: Random House, 1957.

———. *Capitalism: The Unknown Ideal*. New York: New American Library, 1966. See esp. chap. 1, "What Is Capitalism?" and chap. 2, "The Roots of War."

———. "The Comprachicos," in *The New Left: The Anti-Industrial Revolution*, 187–239. New York: Signet, 1975.

———. *For the New Intellectual*. New York: Signet, 1961.

———. *The Fountainhead*. New York: Signet, 1971. First published in 1943.

———. *Introduction to Objectivist Epistemology*, expanded 2nd ed. New York: NAL Books, 1990. First book edition published by Mentor in 1979. Core chapters 1–8 originally published in *The Objectivist*, July 1966–February 1967.

———. "Philosophy and Sense of Life." In *The Romantic Manifesto: A Philosophy of Literature*, 88–121. New York: Signet Books, 1971.

———. *Philosophy: Who needs It*. New York: Bobbs-Merrill, 1982. See esp. chap 1, "Philosophy: Who Needs It"; chap. 3, "The Metaphysical Versus the Man-Made"; chap. 4, "The Missing Link"; and chap. 10, "Causality Versus Duty."

———. *The Virtue of Selfishness: A New Concept of Egoism*. New York: New American Library, 1964. See esp. chap. 1, "The Objectivist Ethics"; chap. 3, "The Ethics of Emergencies"; chap. 7, "Doesn't Life Require Compromise?"; and chap. 12, "Man's Rights."

Rauch, Jonathan. *Kindly Inquisitors: The New Attacks on Free Thought*. Chicago: University of Chicago Press, 1993.

Read, John. "A History of Madness." In *Models of Madness: Psychological, Social and Biological Approaches to Psychosis*, 2nd ed. Edited by John Read and Jacqui Dillon, 9–19. New York: Routledge, 2013. First edition published in 2004.

Read, John, and Jeffrey Masson, "Genetics, Eugenics and Mass Murder." In *Models of Madness: Psychological, Social and Biological Approaches to Psychosis*, 2nd ed. Edited by John Read and Jacqui Dillon, 34–46. New York: Routledge, 2013.

Reardan, Linda. "Emotions as Pleasure/Pain Responses to Evaluative Judgments: A Modern, Aristotelian View" Ph.D. diss., Claremont Graduate University, 1999.

Reisman, George. *Capitalism: A Treatise on Economics*. Laguna Hills, CA: TJS Books, 1996.

Rogers, Carl. *On Becoming a Person: A Therapist's View of Psychotherapy*. New York: Houghton Mifflin, 1961.

Sadofsky, Mimsy, and Daniel Greenberg, eds. *Reflections on the Sudbury School Concept.* Framingham, MA: Sudbury Valley School Press, 1999.

Samenow, Stanton E. *Before It's Too Late: Why Some Kids Get into Trouble—and What Parents Can Do About It.* New York: Three Rivers Press, 2001. First published in 1989.

———. *Inside the Criminal Mind,* rev. ed. New York: Broadway Books, 2014. First edition published in 1984.

———. *The Myth of the "Out of Character" Crime.* Self-published, CreateSpace, 2010. First published in 2007.

———. "Pray at Ten O'Clock, Rob at Noon," *Concept of the Month—March 2014* (blog). http://www.samenow.com/conceptmarch_14.html. Accessed February 8, 2019.

Searle, John R. *Mind: A Brief Introduction.* New York: Oxford University Press, 2004.

Shaw, Julia. *The Memory Illusion: Remembering, Forgetting and the Science of False Memory.* London: Random House Books, 2016.

Smith, George H. *Atheism: The Case Against God.* Buffalo, NY: Prometheus Books, 1989. First published in 1979.

———. "Ayn Rand and Altruism, Part 1," October 23, 2012. https://www.libertarianism.org/publications/essays/excursions/ayn-rand-altruism-part-1.

Stromberg, Joseph. "New Study Shows That Dogs Use Color Vision After All." *Smithsonian.com,* July 17, 2013. https://www.smithsonianmag.com. Search article title.

Szasz, Thomas. *The Ethics of Psychoanalysis: The Theory and Method of Autonomous Psychotherapy.* Syracuse, NY: Syracuse University Press, 1965.

———. "The Myth of Mental Illness." *American Psychologist* 15 (1960): 113–18. https://dx.doi.org/10.1037/h0046535.

———. *The Myth of Mental Illness: Foundations of a Theory of Personal Conduct,* 2nd ed. New York: HarperPerennial, 1974. First edition published in 1961 with the subtitle: *A Critical Assessment of the Freudian Approach.*

Whitaker, Robert. *Anatomy of an Epidemic: Magic Bullets, Psychiatric Drugs, and the Astonishing Rise of Mental illness in America.* New York: Broadway Paperbacks, 2010.

———. *Mad in America: Bad Science, Bad Medicine, and the Enduring Mistreatment of the Mentally Ill.* New York: Basic Books, 2002.

White, Matthew. "Necrometrics: Estimated Totals for the Entire 20th Century," last modified September, 2010. http://necrometrics.com/all20c.htm.

Whitehead, N. E. and B. K. *My Genes Made Me Do It,* 5th ed. (n.p.: Whitehead Associates, 2018). Available for download at http://www.mygenes.co.nz. First edition published in 1999.

Whyte, Lancelot Law. *The Unconscious before Freud: A History of the Evolution of Human Awareness.* New York: Basic Books, 1960.

Windelband, Wilhelm. "Rectorial Address, Strasbourg, 1894." *History and Theory* 19 (February 1980): 169–85.

Wollheim, Richard. *Sigmund Freud.* Cambridge, UK: Cambridge University Press, 1971.

Yochelson, Samuel, and Stanton E. Samenow. *The Criminal Personality.* Vol. 1, *A Profile for Change.* Northvale, NJ: Jason Aronson, 1993., and Vol. 2, *The Change Process.* Northvale, NJ: Jason Aronson, 1994. First published, respectively, in 1976 and 1977.

Zimbardo, Philip. *The Lucifer Effect: Understanding How Good People Turn Evil.* New York: Random House, 2007.

Index

action tendency, 63–64, 87, 150n25, 158
Adler, Alfred, 142n5, 157n37
altruism: and *The Altruistic Personality*, 46; and Kant, 44, 45, 114; and Maslow's self-actualizers, 82; as self-sacrifice, 43–44, 44–47
analytic-synthetic dichotomy, 73n38
Andersen, Hans Christian, 9, 86, 104n31
anecdotal evidence, 74–75, 76–79
anti-conceptual mentality: and dependence, 108–110; and group conformity, 110; and mental passivity, 43, 108
anxiety, objective or normal, 144n8
anxiety, pathological: defensive habits as salve for, 63; as emotional expression of self-doubt, 10, 98; as fear with no apparent object, 91, 100, 143n6; feeling unfit to live, 143
"aristocracy of character, of will, of mind," Ibsen's words, 127n28
Aristotle: and "biological in the Aristotelian sense," 91n12; on essence as in the thing, 75; on identifying cause of desires, 149n23; on formal and efficient causes, 76, 76n46; as founder of psychology, 71; thought revived by Aquinas, 43n64

Asch, Solomon, studies on conformity, 135–36
Ashton, T. S., on the industrial revolution, 23–24
attention deficit hyperactivity disorder (ADHD), 26–27
authoritarianism: as absent from Sudbury Valley School, 28, 106n37; and ADHD, 26; and epistemological certainty, 132–34; and god and religion, 40, 42; in parenting and teaching, 18–19, 110, 164–65; and personal identity, 11; and youth coaches, 162n46
authority, deference to, studies to understand the Holocaust, 135–38
authority, obedience to: and duty, 121, 123; in German child-rearing books, 22–23; and Hobbes, 28; and independence, 11, 18–19, 25–26; meaning of, 37–38; and statism, 52; in traditional schools, 111
automatized versus automatic, 67n28
autonomy: definition of, 124; and independence, 120–25; and individualism, 124–125; and Kant, 120–23

Beck, Aaron, 67n28, 142n5
Beck, Judith S. 67n28, 168n58
behavior, cause of, 61–69

consciousness, volitional: content and orderliness created by humans, 88; denied by determinists, 28; humans free to perform or ignore functions of, 54–55, 64–65
core evaluation. *See* evaluation, core
corporal punishment, 18, 110, 161
creative thinking, opposite of repression, 78n50, 145n10, 180–81;
criminal personality: and crime of passion, 61, 152n29; and dependent personality, 127n27, 134; as dictator, 134; and genetic or biological determinism, 59n15; and habilitation, 71n35; and "jolts of excitement," 59; as liar and cheater, 55; and psychological change, 61; and thinking errors, 59–61

Deci, Edward, on autonomy, 122–23;
defense mechanism, as defensive habit, 47n72
defense value: and anti-conceptual mentality, 109–110; and bragging, 149; and compulsiveness, 148; as pseudo-self-esteem, 110, 147
defensive habit: as helper to repression, 107, 146; as involuntary subconscious response, 145; and suppression, 143, 144;
defensive maneuver: as attempt to assuage anxiety, 107; as behavioral expression of defensive habit, 47n72; as drug high, 108
deism, and god as "scientist in chief," 39
deMause, Lloyd: on history of childhood, 17, 23–24; on standing up to academic critics, 23; "On Writing Childhood History," 23n21
democracy: and capitalism, 114; and rights theory, 116n4, 133; and Socrates, 113, 115;
dependence: and adult acceptance of child's emotions, 161; and autonomy, 124; and behavioral expressions of, 127; and culture of self-sacrifice, 170; and external control psychology, 20; and personal identity, 86; and psychological inhibitions, 55,

106; and religious virtue, 52; and socialism, 105–106;
dependent personality: and anti-conceptual mentality, 43, 108–110; and criminal personality, 127n27, 134; and defense values, 148n20; and fearfulness of others, 100, 104–110; and group conformity, 107–108; and personal identity, 105; as prisoner of childhood, 106–108; and role playing, 127; as "second hander," 104, 104n32; and self-consciousness, 141
depression: and Aaron Beck, 67n28; as choosing to depress, 19; and psychotropic drugs, 33
determinism. *See* materialism and determinism
Dewey, John, 119n13
dictatorship: and the citizen's fear of life, 106; and democracy, 133; and epistemological and ethical certainty, 132–35; and independence, 116–17; and materialism and determinism, 28, 37; root of, 18–21
dreams, 87, 89n8, 156, 180
drugs, psychotropic: actual purpose of, 27; as alleged psychiatric treatment, 29; as harmful, 32–33; and use in hospitals, prisons, schools, 32
duty: as distinguished from obligation, 121n17; and inclination, 44, 46, 118, 121; meaning of, 121; must we die for? 114–15; and salvation, redemption, 44

egoism: and ancient Greeks, 124; and children as "complete egoists," 170; as counterfeit, 122n21; and Enlightenment, 52; fallacy of psychological, 125; and individualism, 70; mutual, 51; of psychology (*see* psychology, egoism of); and self-esteem, 96
electro-convulsive shock, 29, 32
Ellis, Albert, 142n5
emotion: acronym for introspection of, 160n43; catch in the making? 150–51; and core evaluations,

198 • *Index*

independent judgment: and action,
47–48, 85–86, 114, 118, 120, 126,
127, 129–30; as character and
personality trait, 9, 18, 55, 138; and
denigration of, 18: and internal
control psychology, 20; and the
free society 11, 86; meaning of, 9;
and teaching to children, 10; versus
sound judgment, 18, 114, 125;
independent personality: and
capitalism, 103; as guided by facts,
100–104; and internal control
psychology, 104; and introspection,
110; origins and development of,
128, 128n31; as quietly confident,
100; and productive work, 102; as
happy and benevolent, 101–102
individual cases, defense of in science,
76–79
individual differences, and
measurement omission in
formation of concepts, 75
individualism: and autonomy,
120–25; and Comte, 45; and the
Enlightenment, 52; and Glasser,
83; and the industrial revolution,
43n64; as philosophic doctrine,
70; and the Progressives, 36; and
psychoanalysis, 82; of psychology
(*see* psychology, individualism of)
inductive generalization, and
statistical projection, 73
insane asylums: and brutal
treatments, 29–31; as "snake pits,"
34
integration, as maintaining
consistency and adherence to facts,
54
intelligence: analogy to independence,
130; and intervening variables,
130–31; and the less educated, 10,
131; meaning of, 129–30
internal control psychology:
and capitalism, 19, 21; and
independence, 20, 101; and
intrinsic motivation, 19
introspection: and "continuous
defensive observation," 141;
meaning of, 140–41; and mental
health, 95, 97; as valid method of
science, 65, 73n39

introspection, teaching of:
children as speaking in code,
163–64; Goertz and emotional
communication, 164–65; and style
of relating to children, 162–63; and
subject matter, 161–62; workbooks
and worksheets, 166–68

Joseph, Jay: on genes as cause of
behavior, 56–58; on schizophrenia,
58n14
judging people: by external traits,
99, 126–27; through self-report
questionnaires, 127n27

Kant, Immanuel: on autonomy as
voluntary self-sacrifice, 120–21;
on duty to humanity as an end in
itself, 45; on essential formulation
of altruism, 44, 118; as failing to
find "true reality," 74, 114, 117;
and independence, 117–18; and
the "Kantian issue," 117–20;
and relation of consciousness to
existence, 118–119
knowledge, general versus specific,
54, 73
Krüger, J. G., on beating child for
"obstinacy," 22

liberalism, classical: 36, 50n3, 51, 53,
82
logic, Aristotelian: as fundamental
introspective science, 65; as
guide to correct perception of
reality, 65–67, 141; required to
challenge mistaken premises and
conclusions, 66–67
logic, paleo, Arieti's words for illogic
of the subconscious, 89n8
logic, private, words of Adler
followers for normal and neurotic
reasoning, 65n26
logical positivism: as form of
skepticism, 75n43; values
as subjective and science as
probabilistic, 72n37, 74

mad (insane), the, viewed as wild
beasts, 30
Maslow, Abraham: on psychology's

of, 78n50; and contrived studies
on, 77, 77n48; as differentiated
from defense mechanism by Freud,
79n51; and helper defenses, 146;
meaning of, 144–46; memory
researchers on, 89n9; as opposite
of creative thinking, 78n50, 145n10,
180–81
responsibility, existential: as
exercising sound judgment, 126–29,
136; as paying one's bills, 87, 126
responsibility, psychological: as true
independent judgment, 126–29; as
understanding our psychologies, 87
rights: individual, as derived from
human nature as a rational being,
51–52; property, as implementation
of rights to life and liberty, 51
Rogers, Carl, on "unconditional
positive regard," 33
Rome, ancient, and father's right to
kill children, 23

Samenow, Stanton, on criminal
personality, 59–61
sanction: physical, 40–41;
psychological, as more effective
than the physical, 41
schizophrenia: as treated with
psychotropic drugs, 33; World
Health Organization studies on,
33n46
schools, traditional: as controlling
the child, 10; and obedience to
authority, 11, 111
Schreber, D. G. M., on self-
renunciation as proper child-
rearing, 22–23
science: aims and methods of, 72–73;
epistemological balkanization
of, 50; human, as mimicking the
methods of physical science, 76–77;
individual cases in, 73–74
scientism, as pretense at science,
72n36
scientists, as materialists and
determinists, 29, 47, 75
self-defense, principle of, 116–17, 129
self-determination. *See* autonomy
self-doubt: experienced as emotion
of anxiety, 98; localized or normal,
144n8; unacknowledged object and

cause of anxiety, 143n6; opposite of
self-esteem, 143
self-esteem: as cluster of core
and mid-level evaluations, 90;
competence as cognitive, 97;
as degree of confidence about
worthiness and competence, 95–
98; as devalued by the concept of
god, 40; as essential psychological
need, 62; worthiness as egoistic, 96
self-responsibility: as essential
requirement for free society, 86;
as value and virtue, 87. *See also*
independence
self-sacrifice, meaning of, 43–44
selfishness, attributed to
independence, 18. *See also* egoism
Semmelweis, Ignác, and childbed
fever, 29
sense of life: as emotional expression
of core evaluations and self-esteem,
90, 98–99; as implicit metaphysics,
99
shame and humiliation, as induced by
concept of sin, 41, 110n45
sin: as allegedly assuaged by sacrifice,
44; as inducing guilt, 41; as
psychological equivalent of hell, 42
Smith, George H.: on Comte, Ayn
Rand, and altruism, 44–45; on god
and religion, 39–43
social contract: and origin of the
state, 116n4; and Socrates, 115;
socialism, democratic, and the
Progressives, 36
Socrates: death by Hemlock, 10, 113;
executed for independence, 9, 113,
115; refused to go into exile, 115;
and the "Socrates issue," 104n31,
113–17
soul: definitions of Branden and
Freud, 81n56
sound judgment, what most parents
and teachers want, 17–18. *See also*
responsibility, existential
Soviet Union: how some citizens felt
safer there than in freedom, 53;
how some citizens maintained
their independence, 10;
spiritual impoverishment, and the
destruction of self-esteem and
independence, 42

state, administrative: as playing god,
42; and the Progressives, 37
state, the: as god, 42–43, 52; as
omnipotent, 115; origins of, 116n4
statism, as genus of communism,
socialism, and fascism, 52n5
statistical projection (or inference):
and correct place in science,
80n54; as primary method of
logical positivism, 73; versus
scientific induction, 79–80
statistics: superficiality of in the
human sciences, 77, 123, 135; as
collectivizing the individual, 137
subconscious: and automatic
connections not in our control,
88, 90n10; Branden's definition
of, 90n10; content as potentially
conscious and retrievable, 89,
120; and influence on current
behavior, 176; as known from
dreams, creative insight, and
repression, 180–82; meaning
and content of, 178–80; and
memory, 180; as storehouse of
integrated, automatized knowledge
and experiences, 89–90; study
of, cannot be neglected, 176, 181;
versus unconscious, 90n10, 177–78;
von Domarus and Arieti on nature
of, 89n8
Sudbury Valley School: and ADHD,
28; and independence as aim,
106n37
surgery, as psychiatric treatment,
31–32
suppression, as conscious decision to
put out of mind, 144
Szasz, Thomas: on aim of therapy and
(classically) liberal political reform,
82; as critic of the medical model,
35, 35n49; on Freud's greatest
contribution to psychotherapy, 81

talk therapy. *See* psychotherapy
terrible twos, 10, 96
thinking: correct, as required for
mental health and happiness,
49, 54–55, 62, 65; incorrect or
nonexistent, as cause of mental
illness and criminality, 62, 64–65
third force, as Maslow's words for

humanistic psychology, 69–70
trauma, as not repressed or forgotten,
24n25, 145n11, 145n13
truth, theory of, as Rand's
recognition or identification theory,
54n8
truth-telling, when not to, moral
versus practical, 116–17, 129
twin studies: of alleged genetic
influence on behavior, 56–58;
and circular reasoning, 58; and
eugenics, 58n14; as failing to hold
environment constant, 57

unconscious. *See* subconscious
universalization: *See*
conceptualization
universals: scientific search for,
72–81, 76n46, 137; sound theory
of: 74–75, 118–19; 133; *See also*
concepts, Ayn Rand's theory of
unwanted behavior, control of: as
aim of modern psychiatry, 34; by
electroshock, surgery, and drugs,
29; and insane asylums, 30

validity of the senses, 73n38
value, as conclusion of what we
identify as beneficial or harmful,
62
von Domarus, E., 89n8

Western culture, on independence, 17
Whitaker, Robert, as critic of the
medical model, 32–33
Whyte, Lancelot Law: definition of
unconscious, 176n5; on Freud and
Descartes' error, 177; history of the
unconscious, 176

Cover by 1106Design, www.1106Design.com

Interior design by Kirkpatrick Books

Main text: Warnock Pro

Headings: Myriad Pro

CPSIA information can be obtained
at www.ICGtesting.com
Printed in the USA
LVHW110729160919
631184LV00001B/21/P